Costume design by Shelley Norton   *Photo by Beth Lincks*

Greg Steinbruner and Margot White in a scene from
the New York production of *See Rock City*.

SEE ROCK CITY

a sequel to LAST TRAIN TO NIBROC

BY ARLENE HUTTON

★

★

DRAMATISTS
PLAY SERVICE
INC.

SEE ROCK CITY
Copyright © 2006, Arlene Hutton

All Rights Reserved

SPECIAL NOTE

for my aunt and uncle,
Alice and Fred Hutton,
with much love

ACKNOWLEDGMENTS

The playwright wishes to thank 78th Street Theatre Lab, ART/NY, ArtStation, the Australian National Playwrights Conference, Blue Mountain Center, the MacDowell Colony, the Nancy Quinn Fund, New Dramatists, The New Harmony Project, Orlando Playfest, the Vine Theatre, the Virginia Center for the Creative Arts, Yaddo and the Walter E. Dakin Memorial Fund (established at Sewanee: The University of the South, through the estate of the late Tennessee Williams). Also Alexandra Geis and Benim Foster, who originated the roles of May and Raleigh in *Last Train to Nibroc*.

AUTHOR'S NOTE

It has astonished and thrilled me that audiences have responded so enthusiastically to *Last Train to Nibroc* and I've had a good time continuing the story of May and Raleigh.

Like *Last Train to Nibroc*, *See Rock City* plays best when it is staged very simply and with subtlety; both plays are delicate valentines. The characters are good people trying to do their very best in extraordinary circumstances.

It is popular to caricature the people of rural Appalachia, but the story is best told, and actually funnier, if the actors play for truth rather than for laughs. Raleigh is Andy Griffith, not Barney Fife. He is, simply, the nicest guy in the world. There is a type of man I've met over and over again in Kentucky — my father and my Uncle Fred are both such men — who never loses his temper, who reacts to every challenge with gentle humor and who loves life and people with a positive enthusiasm even on the worst of days. Mrs. Gill and Mrs. Brummett are based loosely on my grandmothers. One was a sweet saint loved by all and the other a crotchety woman who saw the world from a very narrow point of view. And May, well, May is the most complex of the four characters. Often she speaks first and thinks later, and her emotions shift too quickly for her own good, but she is always truthful and never actually complaining or whiney. She works hard and she loves her family and her husband.

My father really did paint stripes on a mule. My Uncle Fred told me about his church-going dog. Inspired by my family's stories, I'm continuing the fictional tale of May and Raleigh. Yes, there will be a third play.

Arlene Hutton
The MacDowell Colony
June 2005

SEE ROCK CITY was originally produced by the 78th Street Theatre Lab (Eric Nightengale, Artistic Director; Mark Zeller and Dana Zeller-Alexis, Producing Directors; Ruth Nightengale, General Manager) and The Journey Company (Beth Lincks, Producing Artistic Director) in New York City, opening on February 5, 2004. It was directed by Eric Nightengale; the costume design was by Shelley Norton; the lighting design was by Ji-Youn Chang; and the stage manager was Billie Davis. The cast was as follows:

MAY .... Keri Setaro
RALEIGH .... Greg Steinbruner
MRS. GILL .... Jean Taylor
MRS. BRUMMETT .... Ruth Nightengale

SEE ROCK CITY received full development at The 2004 New Harmony Project in New Harmony, Indiana. It was directed by Eric Nightengale; the dramaturg was Diane Brewer, the literary assistant was Polly Hubbard, the NHP Board Liason was Walt Wangerin and the stage manager was Natalie Bartlett. The cast was as follows:

MAY .... Suzy Hunt
RALEIGH .... Stephen Plunkett
MRS. GILL .... Carrie Preston
MRS. BRUMMETT .... Jan Lucas

A revised version of the play was subsequently produced by the 78th Street Theatre Lab and The Journey Company (Beth Lincks, Producing Artistic Director) in association with the Vine Theatre (Whitney Goin and Stephanie Williams, Artistic Directors) in New York City, opening on March 23, 2005. It was directed by Eric Nightengale; the costume design was by Shelley Norton; the lighting design was by Ji-Youn Chang; and the stage manager was Billie Davis. The cast was as follows:

MAY .... Margot White
RALEIGH .... Greg Steinbruner
MRS. GILL .... Gwendolyn Brown
MRS. BRUMMETT .... Ruth Nightengale

CHARACTERS

MAY — In her twenties. An educated rural schoolteacher.

MRS. GILL — Her mother.

RALEIGH — In his twenties, raised on a sharecrop.

MRS. BRUMMETT — His mother.

Casting Note: The actor playing Raleigh does not have to actually smoke. Where smoking is indicated in the script, the actor can simply be putting out a cigarette as he enters. The casting may be of any color, but all the actors should be the same ethnicity.

PLACE

The front porch of a modest bungalow in eastern Kentucky.

TIME

SCENE ONE: June 1944.
SCENE TWO: a few weeks later.
SCENE THREE: early September 1944.
SCENE FOUR: an hour later.
SCENE FIVE: mid-May 1945.
SCENE SIX: August 1945.

Radio broadcasts of World War II events may be heard between the scenes of the play to give the sense of time passing. This is entirely up to the director; we found that the play works perfectly well without them, using changes in the stage lighting along with big band music from the period. "Mountain music" should be avoided; these characters would prefer swing to bluegrass.

The play is written to be performed without an intermission. However, if one is required, it should be between Scene Four and Scene Five, with Act One taking place in 1944 and Act Two in 1945.

WORLD WAR II TIMELINE RELEVANT TO THE PLAY

1940

Sept. 16: Military conscription introduced in the United States.

1941

Dec. 7: Japanese attack on Pearl Harbor.
Dec. 8: United States and Britain declare war on Japan.
Dec. 11: Germany declares war on the United States.

1944

June 6: D-Day: invasion of Europe begins at Normandy.
June 22: Roosevelt signs the GI bill.
Aug. 25: Paris liberated.
Oct. 2: Allies advance into Germany.

1945

Jan. 16: Battle of the Bulge ends in German defeat.
Jan. 26: Soviets liberate Auschwitz.
Apr. 12: Franklin Delano Roosevelt dies; Truman becomes President.
Apr. 30: Adolf Hitler and wife Eva Braun commit suicide.
May 7: Unconditional surrender of German forces.
May 8: Victory in Europe (VE) Day.
July 16: First U.S. atomic bomb tested at Los Alamos, New Mexico.
Aug. 6: First atomic bomb dropped on Hiroshima.
Aug. 9: Second atomic bomb dropped on Nagasaki.
Aug. 14: Unconditional surrender of Japanese forces.
Aug. 15: Victory over Japan (VJ) Day.

SEE ROCK CITY

SCENE ONE

In the dark we hear radio broadcast reports of the D-Day invasion. Late morning, June, 1944. The front porch of a modest bungalow in a small Kentucky town. Steps lead down to the yard. Stage Left leads towards the side and back yard. Stage Right leads around the house to the driveway, which goes from the road in front toward the back of the house. Downstage faces the main road. Upstage there is an open front door and a closed screen door leading to the front hallway and from there to the living room, right, and the front bedroom, left. On the porch are a small table, chairs, a loveseat and a rocking chair. Presumably the living room leads into a dining room and then into a kitchen, while the hallway center leads to the rest of the house. The set may be realistic or not: There may simply be porch furniture on a bare stage, with the suggestion of a doorway.

Raleigh, carrying a suitcase in each hand, enters from around the driveway side of the house. He puts the suitcases on the porch and stands looking out at the road. He exits back in the direction he came from and reenters, carrying May in his arms. She holds a paper bag and a small red birdhouse with the words "See Rock City" painted in white on the black roof. Raleigh carefully climbs the steps and tries to open the screen door just as Mrs. Gill is coming out. Mrs. Gill wears an apron. Raleigh almost drops May as the door opens.

MAY. We're home!
MRS. GILL. Lawsy day, you give me a fright.
MAY. We're home, Momma.

MRS. GILL. Wasn't expecting your train for another half hour. Your father was just fixing to go meet you. *(Raleigh and May burst out laughing.)*

RALEIGH. We got a lift from Rob Doughty.

MAY. *(To Raleigh.)* Put me down! *(Raleigh feigns dropping May over the porch rail. She screams.)* No! *(Raleigh deposits her in a chair. She sits there with the birdhouse in her lap.)*

RALEIGH. Where's Charlie? I want to tan his hide.

MRS. GILL. He's not here.

MAY. He's gonna catch it when he gets back.

MRS. GILL. His unit shipped out. *(A beat.)*

MAY. Shipped out?

RALEIGH. Already?

MRS. GILL. Day 'fore yesterday.

RALEIGH. Back to Fort —

MRS. GILL. No. To Europe.

MAY. No.

MRS. GILL. They sent him back to Europe.

MAY. Momma!

MRS. GILL. He said for you not to cry. He'll be back before we know it. *(A beat. May is trying not to cry.)*

RALEIGH. I'm sorry, Mrs. Gill.

MAY. How can they send him back? He nearly got killed over there. Hasn't he done enough? You should have sent me a telegram.

MRS. GILL. We did.

MAY. I didn't get to say goodbye.

MRS. GILL. We sent a telegram to your rooming house in Chattanooga. Didn't you get it?

MAY. No. *(A beat. Maybe they look at the birdhouse. Then, quickly overlapping:)*

MRS. GILL. Where are my manners? Would you like something to drink?

RALEIGH. I'll get it, Momma Gill.

MRS. GILL. I've got some lemonade made.

RALEIGH. I'll get it.

MAY. Lemonade! Where'd you get that much sugar? *(Raleigh starts to exit.)*

MRS. GILL. *(Calling after him.)* Raleigh, your mother's on her way over.

RALEIGH. Had to happen. I'll go out back and tell Mr. Gill we're home. *(Raleigh exits into the house.)*

MAY. Momma, I didn't get to say goodbye to —

MRS. GILL. *(Interrupting.)* You didn't bring that birdhouse for me, did you? Maybelle, you didn't dare bring me one of those bird-houses. If I want a birdhouse your father can build me one outa scrap lumber. Don't need to be buying birdhouses.

MAY. It's for Mrs. Brummett. She would have been disappointed if we didn't bring her one. Why'd you invite her over?

MRS. GILL. Maybelle. She's your mother-in-law.

MAY. Doesn't mean I have to like her.

MRS. GILL. Maybelle, Raleigh can hear you.

MAY. He doesn't like her, either. He says she's mean as a snake.

MRS. GILL. Maybelle!

MAY. Well, he does.

MRS. GILL. She's had a hard life. *(Raleigh enters with some glasses and a pitcher of lemonade.)* How was Rock City?

RALEIGH. We didn't get there.

MAY. We didn't get there, Momma. We didn't get to Rock City.

MRS. GILL. What do you mean you didn't get to Rock City?

MAY. We ran out of gasoline.

MRS. GILL. The train ran out of gasoline?

MAY. We didn't make the train.

MRS. GILL. You left in plenty of time. Your father made certain of that.

MAY. Charlie —

RALEIGH. Charlie'd been driving the car all around town the night before he took us to the station.

MAY. Didn't fill up the tank.

RALEIGH. We didn't know it was on empty.

MAY. All the excitement. Didn't think to look at the gauge. The car just stopped. Charlie pretended it broke down. But Raleigh said —

RALEIGH. I said, "Maisy, we are right out of gasoline."

MAY. So Charlie went to find some gasoline.

MRS. GILL. He never said a word about it.

RALEIGH. I just bet he didn't.

MAY. Raleigh and I had to walk the rest of the way. By the time we got to the station the train was already there.

MRS. GILL. So you made it?

RALEIGH. Nope. Thought we were gonna.

MAY. We were racing to catch it and then —

RALEIGH. We were running up the steps to the station.

MAY. And I fell.

11

MRS. GILL. No.

MAY. I was wearing my spectator pumps and my foot just twisted out of the shoe and I fell.

RALEIGH. Twisted her ankle.

MAY. It hurt. So Raleigh picks me up.

RALEIGH. We were gonna make that train, come hell or high water.

MAY. Raleigh!

RALEIGH. Well, we were. So I say, "May, grab a suitcase."

MAY. And I grab the little suitcase and he picks me up and I'm holding onto his neck with one hand and the suitcase with the other and he picks up the other suitcase and nearly drops me.

RALEIGH. I was just rearrangin' you to get my balance.

MAY. You almost dropped me.

RALEIGH. I did not.

MAY. Did so. And we run for the train, me holding on to one suitcase and my purse and Raleigh carrying me and the other suitcase and the train pulled out of the station!

MRS. GILL. Mercy me!

RALEIGH. And then you —

MAY. Then I what?

RALEIGH. Then you —

MAY. You set me down on a bench.

RALEIGH. Before that.

MAY. Oh, well, of course I started crying.

RALEIGH. So the stationmaster takes pity on us and changes the ticket.

MAY. So we got on the next train.

RALEIGH. In the other direction.

MAY. We went to Cincinnati.

MRS. GILL. Cincinnati!

MAY. That's why we didn't get the telegram.

MRS. GILL. If you didn't get to Rock City, then where did you get the "See Rock City" birdhouse?

RALEIGH. Well, my mom's always wanted one of those birdhouses. And next to our rooming house in Cincinnati, there just happens to be this man hanging a brand-new birdhouse from his tree.

MRS. GILL. No.

MAY. Yes! There was! Right next door.

RALEIGH. So I go over and say, mister, I'll give you a dollar for that birdhouse.

MAY. And *he* says —

12

RALEIGH. *(To May.)* I don't recollect you hoppin' over there with me.

MAY. I was watching from the window. *(To Mrs. Gill.)* I had to keep my ankle up.

RALEIGH. And he says, that he's not in the birdhouse business. Well, I can't hardly keep from laughing, 'cause he's being so serious about our transaction. When I finally catch my breath I tell him my momma wants a birdhouse real bad.

MAY. Raleigh was trying so hard not to laugh, his face was turning red.

RALEIGH. And he says, son, I don't like making birdhouses and if I let you have this birdhouse I'm gonna have t' make another one. And I'm biting my lip just to keep from laughing in his face, 'cause he's so serious. And I nod, like I understand how hard it is to make a birdhouse, and I look down at the ground for a minute, shaking my head all sad like, and I look at the birdhouse again, like I'm thinkin' real hard and then I look that old man in the face. I tell him, Mister, I'll give you *two* dollars for that birdhouse if you'll paint "See Rock City" on the roof of it and sell it to me. And that feller looks me up and down and says "mighty expensive birdhouse, son. But if you're just stupid enough to pay two dollars for it, well, then I'm just smart enough to sell it to you." So my mom's gonna have her birdhouse with "See Rock City" on it.

MAY. Should've said "See Cincinnati"!

MRS. GILL. "See Cincinnati"! *(Some forced laughter and then a pause.)* So did you get to see Cincinnati? With your swollen ankle?

MAY. Raleigh saw Cincinnati. I saw the rooming house. Raleigh went exploring all over the town and wrote about everything he saw and everyone he met. He'd put it all down in a little notebook and then he'd come back to our room and read it to me and make it into stories.

RALEIGH. And while I'd be out havin' adventures, guess what May was doin'.

MRS. GILL. What?

RALEIGH. She was gradin' my stories.

MAY. Was not.

RALEIGH. Was so. Think all those little marks were ants marching across the paper?

MAY. I didn't give you a grade. I was just helping with your punctuation.

RALEIGH. Well, maybe I don't like all those commas you put in.

Looks like a lot of little ants curled up and dying on my story. Makes me think the ants don't like my writing. *(May laughs a little. Mrs. Gill smiles. Raleigh gives May a peck on the top of her head. Mrs. Gill looks out toward the road. There is a pause.)*

MAY. Did you find Daddy?

RALEIGH. He's yonder back in his workshop.

MRS. GILL. Don't know what I'm gonna do with him. He moved the radio out to his workshop. Spends all his time back there these days. Drawing up floorplans. Says he's planning to build a house for the two of you as soon as the war's over.

MAY. A house.

MRS. GILL. Spends all his time in his workshop. Listening to the radio. Since the invasion I can't get him away from that radio. Raleigh, there's some mail for you on the table.

RALEIGH. Thanks. *(Raleigh takes the suitcases and the birdhouse inside.)*

MRS. GILL. *(To May.)* You left your bedroom a mess.

MAY. Momma!

MRS. GILL. You should be keeping house better now. You're a married woman.

MAY. I know, Momma.

MRS. GILL. Well, I've got to finish the sandwiches. Mrs. Brummett's on her way over to say hello.

MAY. I'll set the table.

MRS. GILL. It's cooler outside. We'll have them out here on the porch. How's your ankle?

MAY. Still swollen. It'll be a few days before I can drive again.

MRS. GILL. Just rest yourself. *(Raleigh reenters as Mrs. Gill starts to leave with the lemonade pitcher.)* Raleigh, nice that your momma's able to stop by.

RALEIGH. Yep.

MAY. We can give her the birdhouse.

RALEIGH. Yep.

MRS. GILL. I'm sure she'll like it.

MAY. Oh, I almost forgot your present, Momma! *(May hands Mrs. Gill the paper bag.)*

MRS. GILL. Didn't have to spend your money on me.

MAY. Thought you'd like this. *(Mrs. Gill pulls a linen dish towel from the bag and holds it up. It has flowers on it and says "Cincinnati" in big letters.)*

MRS. GILL. Well, that's just the prettiest tea towel I've ever seen.

Thank you very much. Raleigh, if you'll do the churning we'll have us some ice cream later.

MAY. Ice cream!

MRS. GILL. Charlie left us some extra ration coupons. I've made us a peach cobbler, too.

RALEIGH. Peach cobbler and ice cream? Sounds mighty fine to me. *(Mrs. Gill goes inside the house. There is a moment of silence. A car drives by. Looking out:)* Studebaker. Remember that old Studebaker, May? *(Raleigh starts to kiss May as Mrs. Brummett comes around the corner of the house, carrying a covered pie plate.)*

MRS. BRUMMETT. Raleigh Brummett, the neighbors can see you.

RALEIGH. Hello, Mom.

MRS. BRUMMETT. *(Confidentially to May.)* I'm surprised at you, young lady. You're a school principal. You've gotta stay respectable. Them boys cain't help themselves. But you can. Did your momma ever have a talk with you?

MAY. Yes, she did, Mrs. Brummett.

MRS. BRUMMETT. You should be calling me Mom Brummett by now.

MAY. Well, I reckon I should.

RALEIGH. Mom.

MRS. BRUMMETT. *(To Raleigh.)* Remember, you're married to a respectable girl, even if she is a Methodist. You treat her with respect.

RALEIGH. Yes, Mom.

MRS. BRUMMETT. You don't want her to ever regret marryin' you.

RALEIGH. No, Mom.

MRS. BRUMMETT. *(To May.)* I've been meanin' to ask you to join us at the Baptist church some Sunday. *(To Raleigh.)* Never regretted marryin' your daddy. Not once. *(To May.)* We had a nice weddin', too. With a fiddler. We had a fiddler. *(Raleigh puts his finger in the pie and tastes it.)*

MAY. *(To Mrs. Brummett.)* Mrs ... Mom Brummett. We brought you a —

MRS. BRUMMETT. *(To Raleigh.)* Have you been goin' to church?

RALEIGH. Whenever I can, Mom. *(To May.)* Peach cobbler.

MAY. Raleigh, I'm gonna go inside and get your momma's present.

RALEIGH. I'll get it. You rest your ankle. *(Raleigh exits with the pie. May is now alone with Mrs. Brummett.)*

MRS. BRUMMETT. You shouldn't've spent nothin' on me.

MAY. Had to get you a little something. *(A pause.)*

MRS. BRUMMETT. It'll be mighty nice when you have your

15

own house.

MAY. Yes, it will.

MRS. BRUMMETT. You make good money teachin' school?

MAY. Reckon it's enough.

MRS. BRUMMETT. Well, I just want to tell you I'm sorry you have to be a'workin' all the time. *(May starts to speak and thinks better of it.)* Someday that boy Raleigh will wake up and get a job and then you can stay home in your own house with your own babies. Just wanted to let you know I understand about husbands and such and if you ever want to talk I'll be happy to give you my ear.

MAY. Raleigh has a job, Mrs. Brummett.

MRS. BRUMMETT. *(Correcting her.) Mom* Brummett.

MAY. Raleigh has a job. He's a writer.

MRS. BRUMMETT. Hmph. I mean a real job.

MAY. Raleigh sells his stories to national magazines. They pay him. They pay him as much for one story as I get for a whole semester.

MRS. BRUMMETT. Not regular. They don't pay him regular.

MAY. No, it's not a regular paycheck. But he makes money writing. He's a good writer.

MRS. BRUMMETT. My son-in-law Harold had a regular job up in Dee-troit. On the assembly line. Dee-fense job. Paycheck every week. Till he got called up t' the service.

MAY. Yes, I know.

MRS. BRUMMETT. That Harold, he's a worker. My daughter Treva, too. Runnin' our farm nearly by herself, me lookin' after them two babies for her. Raleigh never did work hard. Always had to keep pushin' him. You'd give 'm someth'n to do and he'd start doin' it and then suddenly he'd be just starin' inta space. Just a dreamin' all the time. Watchin' people. Dreamin' up pranks. Always gettin' inta trouble. The thangs that boy would do. Why, he'd throw dirt up in the air outside the fan at the movie house. Said he wanted to see what would happen to the dirt. Got sucked in all over the people in the movie house is what it did. He got a whuppin' for that, I can tell you. I don't want you to think that I raised him to be so lazy. He got whipped mor'n any child I ever know'd. I cut so many switches to whup him with, that we ran out of bushes. Had to use my hairbrush or Mr. Brummett's belt. But all that pushin' an' whuppin' didn't make a worker outa him. Always just havin' fun. Nothin' bothers that boy. *(Mrs. Gill and Raleigh enter. He carries a pitcher of lemonade.)*

MRS. GILL. Hello, Mrs. Brummett.

MRS. BRUMMETT. Miz Gill. Nice to see you.

MRS. GILL. You're just in time for lemonade.

MRS. BRUMMETT. *(To Raleigh.)* Raleigh, you workin' in the kitchen these days?

RALEIGH. The women in this house won't let me near the kitchen, Mom. Guess I'm just the waitress.

MAY. *(To Mrs. Brummett.)* My ankle's swollen. *(To Mrs. Gill.)* Thanks, Momma.

MRS. BRUMMETT. *(To Mrs. Gill.)* Miz Gill, you didn't need to go to no trouble on my account.

MRS. GILL. No trouble.

MRS. BRUMMETT. I heerd your son was called back up.

MRS. GILL. Yes, he was. Left day before yesterday.

MRS. BRUMMETT. The Lord works in mysterious ways.

MRS. GILL. Yes, He does.

MRS. BRUMMETT. Good thing your son wasn't on that train down to Jellico.

MAY. What train?

RALEIGH. Jumped the tracks by the gorge.

MAY. How'd you know that?

RALEIGH. Porter told me. When I was getting our bags off.

MRS. BRUMMETT. Jumped right off the tracks.

MRS. GILL. We just heard it on the radio.

MRS. BRUMMETT. A thousand soldiers on that train. Jumped right off the tracks. Inta Clear Fork River. Good thing your boy wasn't on it.

MRS. GILL. Yes.

MAY. Raleigh, would you get —

RALEIGH. Yep. *(Raleigh exits back into the house.)*

MRS. BRUMMETT. They're sayin' a dozen boys were killt.

MRS. GILL. It's a blessing there weren't more.

MRS. BRUMMETT. It's a blessin' your boy weren't on that train.

MRS. GILL. Would you like some more lemonade?

MRS. BRUMMETT. Blessin' there weren't more killt than that.

MRS. GILL. Thank you for bringing us a pie.

MRS. BRUMMETT. You're mighty welcome.

MRS. GILL. You know, Mr. Gill's been asking for a peach cobbler.

MRS. BRUMMETT. Our peaches are early this year.

MRS. GILL. Well, that's just lovely. Thank you very much.

MRS. BRUMMETT. Using a little honey stretches out the sugar ration.

MRS. GILL. What a good idea. *(Raleigh brings out the birdhouse.)*
RALEIGH. Look at this, Mom!
MRS. BRUMMETT. Well, what about that! You brung Miz Gill a Rock City birdhouse.
MAY. It's for you, Mrs. Brummett.
MRS. BRUMMETT. For me?
RALEIGH. Yep, Mom. You said you always wanted one.
MRS. BRUMMETT. Well, now!
MRS. GILL. Isn't that pretty!
MRS. BRUMMETT. *(To Mrs. Gill.)* They brought us birdhouses.
MRS. GILL. Oh, no. They brought me a nice tea towel.
MRS. BRUMMETT. That's not a — Miz Gill, you should have the birdhouse.
MRS. GILL. They brought it just for you, Mrs. Brummett.
RALEIGH. *(Overlapping.)* It's for you, Mom.
MAY. *(Overlapping.)* Raleigh picked it out just for you.
MRS. BRUMMETT. Ain't nobody to see it where we are. We're not on a main road, back where we are, back in the holler.
MAY. *You* will see it, Mrs. Brummett. And the birds.
MRS. BRUMMETT. Well, I always wanted one of them birdhouses.
MRS. GILL. And now you have one!
MRS. BRUMMETT. *(Aside, to Raleigh.)* If you couldn't afford two birdhouses you shouldn't have bought any. Miz Gill should've got one, too. Dish towel. That's not a proper gift. You're livin' in Miz Gill's house. You should've got —
MAY. *(Overlapping.)* It's a pretty tea towel.
MRS. GILL. Oh, yes! With a picture of —
RALEIGH. *(Overlapping, realizing that the tea towel has a picture of Cincinnati on it.)* Real nice flowers on it.
MAY. It's very pretty.
MRS. BRUMMETT. It's not a birdhouse.
MRS. GILL. No, it isn't. But it was a perfect gift. I needed a new tea towel. *(Changing the subject.)* Would you like some more lemonade, Mrs. Brummett? Your glass looks empty.
MRS. BRUMMETT. If I drink any more I'll have to swim home. *(To May.)* Did you like Rock City?
MAY. Um … we … we had a wonderful vacation, Mrs … Mom Brummett!
MRS. BRUMMETT. *(Shaking her head.)* Takin' a vacation when there's a war on.

18

MAY. Raleigh just got paid for six of his stories.

RALEIGH. Mom, May never got a honeymoon last year.

MRS. BRUMMETT. *(To Raleigh.)* Your Aunt Dora went to Rock City on her honeymoon. Said you can see seven states from Lookout Mountain. Can you really see seven states?

RALEIGH. Sure can.

MAY. *(Overlapping.)* It was too hazy to see.

RALEIGH. They say you can see seven states on a clear day.

MRS. BRUMMETT. That's too bad. Go all the way to Rock City and don't even see the seven states. Did you see Lover's Leap?

RALEIGH. Nearly jumped off it!

MAY. Did not!

MRS. BRUMMETT. Always wanted to see Rock City. Was there —

RALEIGH. *(Cutting her off.)* Mom, we don't want to tell you too much, because May and I want to take you there sometime!

MAY. Oh, yes.

MRS. BRUMMETT. Oh, you should take Miz Gill. You're livin' in her home.

MRS. GILL. No! I'm afraid of heights. I'd get dizzy lookin' down on seven states.

MRS. BRUMMETT. You could git yourself a birdhouse.

RALEIGH. They sell them in the gift shop. All sizes. There's little biddy one's, too. People use 'em as ornaments on their Christmas trees.

MAY. Raleigh!

RALEIGH. That's what the lady in the gift shop said.

MAY. And just when did you talk to the lady in the gift shop?

RALEIGH. When do you think? While you were restin' your ankle back at the —

MAY. Oh, yes! *(To Mrs. Brummett.)* I twisted my ankle.

MRS. BRUMMETT. *(To May.)* You hurt yourself on them rocks?

RALEIGH. Well, like we said, it was a cloudy day. And this fine little drizzle starts fallin'. Those are the slipp'riest rocks when they get wet.

MAY. Raleigh!

MRS. BRUMMETT. *(To Raleigh.)* You should've been careful. You've never been careful.

MRS. GILL. I'll go tell Mr. Gill we're having lunch on the porch. Would you like to come in and see the quilt top I'm piecing, Mrs. Brummett?

MRS. BRUMMETT. Yes, I would. And I need to use the … your

facility.

MRS. GILL. Then come on inside. It's at the end of the hall.

MRS. BRUMMETT. *(To Raleigh.)* Inside. You are really livin', ain't ya? I hope you're being nice to these folk. And mindin' your manners. You better be doing what Miz Gill tells you to do. You're not so old that I cain't take a switch to you. *(Mrs. Gill and Mrs. Brummett exit into the house.)*

MAY. Your momma was telling me what a bad boy you were. Always up to something.

RALEIGH. *(Tongue-in-cheek.)* I'm serious now. Not up to anything.

MAY. Best not be, with your momma right inside. *(Raleigh tickles May.)* You're gonna get into trouble.

RALEIGH. My fun days are over, I reckon.

MAY. Did you get spanked a lot?

RALEIGH. You wantin' to spank me about something, May?

MAY. *(Laughing.)* Did your parents spank you a lot?

RALEIGH. Every single day, felt like. Yours?

MAY. Not that I recollect. Well, no, maybe when I was real little and started to run out in the street or something dangerous like that. Charlie was the one always getting into trouble. *(A pause.)*

RALEIGH. Charlie will be back before you know it. And we'll play some tricks on him for a change.

MAY. I thought he was home for good. How could they send him back so soon?

RALEIGH. Guess Uncle Sam's playing a trick on Charlie, bringing him home and then sending him back again. But think of all the good stories he'll have for us.

MAY. Tell me a story.

RALEIGH. Right now?

MAY. Tell me a story.

RALEIGH. You've heard all my stories, May.

MAY. Tell me about when your momma spanked you.

RALEIGH. Lotta stories there, I reckon. *(Raleigh suddenly laughs.)*

MAY. What?

RALEIGH. Nothin'. Just remembering something.

MAY. What? Tell me.

RALEIGH. You remember Dimwit Danny?

MAY. Sure.

RALEIGH. 'Member how he had that ole white mule? That ole white mule and a buckboard?

MAY. What about it?

RALEIGH. 'Member how Dimwit used to meet the train every day and carry people's luggage? He'd sit on the bench outside Stewie's, napping. That ole mule in the back, hitched to the buckboard? That mule would know exactly what time it was and just before the train was due would come 'round to the front of Stewie's and stand there in front of Dimwit Danny waitin' to go to the station and meet the train.

MAY. I don't remember that.

RALEIGH. Well, I sure do. That mule would stay in the back lot behind the store until he knew it was time to go meet the train.

MAY. My daddy's mules were never that smart.

RALEIGH. Well, one day, I take a bucket of black paint and a paintbrush and while Dimwit Danny is nappin' in out front of Stewie's I go around t' the back and paint black stripes on that ole white mule.

MAY. You do what?

RALEIGH. I paint black stripes on that old white mule.

MAY. Why on earth would you do a thing like that?

RALEIGH. Wanted to see what a zebra looked like.

MAY. A what?

RALEIGH. A zebra. In school we're reading all about Africa and I can't figure out what a zebra would look like. So I paint stripes on that ol' mule and then I stand back and look at it and I say to myself, well, so that's what a zebra looks like!

MAY. You didn't.

RALEIGH. Did, too. And my momma nearly whupped me for it.

MAY. I just bet she did. How'd she find out?

RALEIGH. Well, about the time I finish paintin' stripes on him, the mule knows it's time to wake up Dimwit to go meet the train, so that striped mule takes off headin' 'round to the front of Stewie's. And I follow after him because I want to imagine what a *moving* zebra looks like, with the stripes moving an' all. And ever'body on Main Street stops in their tracks when they see this zebra-striped mule and they laugh and point and laugh and Dimwit just can't figure out how his mule has stripes all of a sudden. Somebody sees me with the paint bucket and runs tells my daddy. Well, after supper my momma takes me to Dimwit's house — he lived with his sister — and my momma drags me up the steps and knocks on the door. When Dimwit opens it, my momma tells him that I have somethin' to say to him. So I tell Dimwit how I painted stripes on his mule because I wanted to see what a zebra looked like and that my momma is gonna whoop me for it. And Dimwit, he looks at me, and then he looks at my momma and he says to my momma that I didn't mean no harm. And for her not to punish me. And my momma has to promise that she won't lay a hand on me.

MAY. Reckon Dimwit wasn't such a dimwit after all.

RALEIGH. Reckon he wasn't. *(A pause.)*

MAY. Did you really paint stripes on a mule?

RALEIGH. Sure did.

MAY. And he stood there and let you do it?

RALEIGH. I think he liked the attention.

MAY. Sounds like something Charlie would have done. *(May lays her head on Raleigh's shoulder. He puts his arm around her. Mrs. Gill appears in the doorway.)*

MRS. GILL. Your father wants to eat inside.

MAY. We'll be right there, Momma.

MRS. GILL. Did you see your mail, Raleigh?

RALEIGH. Yes, thank you.

MRS. GILL. You got a lot of mail.

RALEIGH. Sure did.

MRS. GILL. Lunch is on the table. *(Mrs. Gill goes back inside, carrying the tray with the glasses and lemonade. May calls after her.)*

MAY. We'll be right there, Momma. *(To Raleigh, eagerly.)* You look at your mail?

RALEIGH. Yep.

MAY. Sell some more stories to the magazines?

RALEIGH. Nope.

MAY. No?

RALEIGH. Not one. All rejection letters.

MAY. You're teasing me. What did you sell?

RALEIGH. Not a thing. Not one story.

MAY. You'll sell one next week.

RALEIGH. May, I haven't sold a story in four months. *(A pause.)*

MAY. What do you mean? You just got paid for a whole bunch of stories.

RALEIGH. I got the checks for a bunch of stories that I sold last year.

MAY. You get lots of mail.

RALEIGH. Lots of rejections.

MAY. I don't understand. Those magazine editors used to buy everything you'd send them.

RALEIGH. Nothing's selling right now.

MAY. You're mailing out new stories every week.

RALEIGH. Yep.

MAY. At the post office they're always teasing me that you've got a girlfriend in New York City that you're sending mail to.

RALEIGH. Only girlfriend I've got is right here. It'll be all right, Maisy. Everything's under control.

MAY. Last time you said that we missed the train. *(May squeals as Raleigh picks her up and carries her inside the house. The lights change.)*

SCENE TWO

In the transition we hear radio broadcasts, or swing era music. A few weeks later. Raleigh comes out on the porch, newspaper, mail and a magazine in his hand. He sits and stares out. May enters from the house. She wears an apron.

MAY. I hate cooking.

RALEIGH. Let your momma do it. She loves to cook.

MAY. I've gotta learn sometime. *(She picks up the newspaper.)* Who died now?

RALEIGH. May.

MAY. Just seems like every one of my students has lost a father or a brother. It's hard to take.

RALEIGH. Lot of action in the Pacific.

MAY. Then I'm glad Charlie's not there. Do you think he was in the Invasion?

RALEIGH. No, May, I don't. I think they must've sent all the new boys to Normandy. I bet you a dollar that Charlie's in Africa. Someplace real interesting like that.

MAY. Well, I don't know how you can read the newspaper anymore. Too much bad news.

RALEIGH. Something interesting today. Some good news. Real good news.

MAY. What? Tell me.

RALEIGH. They've got this new thing, this new law, a bill, actually. The GI bill. And you can go to college for free.

MAY. I've already been to college.

RALEIGH. No. Me.

MAY. Why would you want to go to college? You're smarter than anyone I know.

RALEIGH. To get an education.

MAY. Think you're gonna read more books in college than you already do now? Just four years of busywork.

RALEIGH. I could get a degree.

MAY. What d'you need a degree for? Don't need it to write stories. You only need a degree if you want to teach.

RALEIGH. Well, maybe I'd like to teach.

MAY. Oh.

RALEIGH. Wouldn't you like that, May? We could both be teachers.

MAY. Can't teach just anywhere. What if you got a job in one state and I was in another?

RALEIGH. We'd have to work that out.

MAY. You expect me to go with you just wherever you got a job?

RALEIGH. Hadn't thought about it.

MAY. Reckon not.

RALEIGH. So you wouldn't want me to try to make teacher?

MAY. Just don't think it's practical.

RALEIGH. Prob'bly not, May. I guess you're the teacher in this family. *(A pause.)*

MAY. I've got to finish making this pie.

RALEIGH. What's it gonna be?

MAY. Lemon meringue.

RALEIGH. Okay.

MAY. Your momma's recipe.

RALEIGH. Good. *(A car drives by. Looking out:)* DeSoto.

MAY. I know her food's better than mine.

RALEIGH. Just what I'm used to, May. I'll get used to your food. Just take me a little while. Like in the service. Took a while to get used to the food in the mess hall.

MAY. Your momma says you're losing weight.

RALEIGH. And I thought I was getting fat, sitting around here!

MAY. Don't be silly. *(She sniffs the air.)* Oh, no. It's burning! I've burned the pie. *(May runs into the house. Raleigh pulls a form out from under his magazine and starts writing. Mrs. Gill enters from the side yard with the mail. She hands it to Raleigh.)*

MRS. GILL. Reckon some iced tea would taste nice.

RALEIGH. Sure would.

MRS. GILL. I've got some made. *(She exits into the house. Raleigh sorts through the mail, making two separate piles. He glances at each of the letters in his pile but leaves them on the table, unopened. From inside the house:)* Do you need any help?

MAY. *(From inside the house.)* No, Momma. Everything's under control.

MRS. GILL. *(From inside the house.)* That oven burns hot.

MAY. *(From inside the house.)* I know, Momma. *(Mrs. Gill reenters with two glasses of iced tea and puts one in front of Raleigh.)*

RALEIGH. Thank you.

MRS. GILL. Lotta mail for you.

RALEIGH. Yep.

MRS. GILL. Aren't you gonna open them?

RALEIGH. Later. They're just rejection letters. That's all I've been getting lately, rejection letters.

MRS. GILL. You've had so many stories published. Reckon they'd be taking everything you write now.

RALEIGH. That's all changed.

MRS. GILL. How's that?

RALEIGH. They want stories about soldiers, about the war. About Europe. About islands in the Pacific. They don't want stories about Kentucky folk.

MRS. GILL. Then write about soldiers. *(A pause.)*

RALEIGH. Already too many boys writing from the frontlines. You have to be there and see the war firsthand to make it authentic. I just sit here and imagine what it's like. Never been there, so I don't know how to write about it. I can only write about what I know. And all I know is about staying home when everyone else is off fighting. And no one wants to read about that.

MRS. GILL. I reckon you got yourself a problem.

RALEIGH. Reckon so. *(They sit in silence for a moment. Mrs. Gill reads the newspaper. A car drives by. Looking out:)* Chrysler.

MRS. GILL. You could write about automobiles. *(Raleigh doesn't speak.)* You don't go into town much these days, do you? Don't take Maybelle to the pictures.

RALEIGH. May's busy. She's gettin' ready for school to start. When she's not in meetin's she's always fillin' out forms and such.

MRS. GILL. You don't even go to church with us anymore. *(A pause.)*

RALEIGH. I don't like going into town. People stare at me, 'cause I'm not in uniform. They whisper. Little boys throw rocks at me and call me a coward. I wanted to go fight — volunteered, even — I'd still go fight if they'd let me, but they won't. I haven't had a

25

seizure in over a year. Over a year. And they still won't let me go.

MRS. GILL. You could write about that. *(A pause.)* I'd better go drag Mr. Gill away from his radio. *(Mrs. Gill exits through the side yard. Raleigh takes out his form.)*

MAY. *(Calling from inside the house.)* Momma? Momma! *(Raleigh hurriedly puts the form under a magazine and lays both on a table. He picks up a book and pretends to read.)*

RALEIGH. She's gone out in the back to fetch your daddy.

MAY. *(From inside the house.)* Then you come look at this pie.

RALEIGH. I know what a pie looks like.

MAY. Well, goody for you. Then come in here and tell me if this is what a pie is supposed to look like. *(May opens the door and comes onto the porch, holding the door for Raleigh. She wears an apron and a scowl and carries a tea towel.)*

RALEIGH. You are fixin' to leave soon, aren't you? You didn't forget about the birthday party, did you?

MAY. What do you think I've been doin' in the kitchen? Think I'm makin' a pie just for you? Why'd I ever say I'd bring a pie, a meringue pie to boot. Go look at it. Hurry up. And don't hold the door open. You'll let the flies in.

RALEIGH. They won't eat much.

MAY. Get in the kitchen and look at that pie. Tell me if that looks like a lemon meringue pie to you.

RALEIGH. Can't tell by lookin'. *(As he exits into the house.)* Gonna have to taste it.

MAY. *(Calling after him.)* Don't you dare touch that pie! Just look at it! Don't touch it! *(May swats a fly and sits down. May picks up the magazine but doesn't notice the form underneath. She glances at the magazine and puts it back down, just as Raleigh comes back out. He sees her put down the magazine but doesn't know if she saw the paper under it or not.)* Did you see the pie? *(Raleigh puts his head down, and clasps his hands below his waist, looking like he's at a funeral.)*

RALEIGH. That's a mighty sad-looking pie, Maisie.

MAY. It's supposed to be fluffy. *(Raleigh doesn't speak.)* With a three-inch meringue.

RALEIGH. *(After a pause.)* What kind of pie did you say it was?

MAY. You can't tell?

RALEIGH. Sometimes it's hard to tell what a pie is until you cut into it.

MAY. It's a lemon meringue pie.

RALEIGH. Oh.

MAY. It's supposed to be fluffy.

RALEIGH. They usually are.

MAY. But it's flat.

RALEIGH. I could see that.

MAY. I can't take that to your daddy's birthday. What am I gonna do? Your momma gave me the recipe. I told her how much I liked her pie and she said it was your daddy's favorite, so I thought I'd take one to him for his birthday. Saved up the sugar and everything.

RALEIGH. That's why my cornbread's been so sour every morning. You've been rationing the sugar from my cornbread.

MAY. Still didn't have enough for the recipe.

RALEIGH. That'll be a sour pie, then. Makes me pucker up just thinking about it. *(Raleigh purses his lips and starts to kiss May. She swats at him in fun.)*

MAY. I'm busy.

RALEIGH. Thinking about that pie makes me hungry. Let's get going. *(May sits down.)*

MAY. What'm I gonna do? I don't have time to make another pie. And even if I did make another pie, there's no guarantee it would be better. Doesn't look like any lemon meringue pie I've ever seen.

RALEIGH. It's not a lemon meringue pie, that's for sure.

MAY. I feel so stupid.

RALEIGH. Call it something else.

MAY. What?

RALEIGH. Did you taste the filling?

MAY. Yes.

RALEIGH. And it tasted fine.

MAY. It was all right. Tasted lemony.

RALEIGH. You don't have to tell anyone it was supposed to be a meringue pie. Call it a … a … a Flat Pie. A Lemony Flat Pie. Tell everyone it's a recipe you found. It's a Lemony Flat Pie. So that problem's solved. Let's go. *(Raleigh pulls May to her feet.)*

MAY. What if someone asks me for the recipe?

RALEIGH. You can tell them it's secret.

MAY. And if your daddy asks me to make it again?

RALEIGH. Why don't you cross that bridge when you come to it. Might not come up.

MAY. You mean no one will ask me to make it again.

RALEIGH. I didn't say that.

MAY. Uh-huh.

RALEIGH. Don't be putting words into my mouth.

MAY. You are just too clever for your own good.

RALEIGH. But I'm clever for your good. *(Raleigh bends to kiss her neck. May ducks, then giggles and lets him embrace her. He goes to kiss her again, and she ducks, teasing him and bumping into the table. The papers fall off. May picks them up and sees the form.)*

MAY. What's this?

RALEIGH. What's what?

MAY. This.

RALEIGH. Nothin'. Somethin' I was lookin' at. I'll tell you later. Let's pack up your pie and get on the road.

MAY. You've been filling out an application.

RALEIGH. Just thinking about it.

MAY. You've filled in most of the spaces.

RALEIGH. Neat handwritin', don't you think?

MAY. You be serious, now. What is this?

RALEIGH. It's just a —

MAY. It's an application. It's an application for Union College in Barbourville. It's an application for college.

RALEIGH. Is it? I thought it was one of those contests. In twenty-five words or less …

MAY. You applying to college?

RALEIGH. Thought I might win the contest. *(May hits him with the paper.)*

MAY. You be serious.

RALEIGH. I am serious.

MAY. No. You tell me what this is about. You be serious with me.

RALEIGH. I am serious. I'm applyin' to college.

MAY. And you weren't gonna tell me?

RALEIGH. Just got the application. Didn't have time to tell you.

MAY. You didn't have time? You had time to fill out this form.

RALEIGH. Maisy, honey, you were bakin' a pie. I know better than to disturb you when you're in the kitchen. Been chased out of there often enough. *(Raleigh puts his arm around her. She pushes him off.)*

MAY. Wait a minute. I'm mad at you!

RALEIGH. How can you be mad at me? I just told how to fix your pie.

MAY. But you didn't tell me about the application.

RALEIGH. I was planning to.

MAY. Planning to when? When you get accepted? When you start school? Or were you just gonna invite me to the graduation? Surprise! Guess what!

RALEIGH. I haven't applied. Just thinkin' about it.

MAY. How are you gonna get there for classes?

RALEIGH. Well, now, that's a problem, May. But I thought I'd cross that bridge when I came to it and not worry about things before they happen.

MAY. You never plan ahead, do you. Just take it as it comes.

RALEIGH. Sometimes that's best.

MAY. Just, "Oh, let's get married tonight." Or "I think I'll take a train to New York City." Or "I'll volunteer for the service."

RALEIGH. Applying to college is planning ahead.

MAY. But we should talk it over.

RALEIGH. We are talkin' it over.

MAY. Before you applied.

RALEIGH. I haven't applied yet.

MAY. But you're going to.

RALEIGH. Don't know yet. Thought we should talk it over. So let's talk it over and then I'll decide whether to apply or not.

MAY. You just ... you just ...

RALEIGH. See, we're talkin' it over before I apply. Just like you want. *(May can't help herself. She bursts out laughing.)*

MAY. You are something else. You're just a ... just a ... big ... a big boy.

RALEIGH. You'd rather me be a big girl?

MAY. *(Laughing.)* Stop. Let's talk serious.

RALEIGH. You, first. *(May can't stop laughing.)*

MAY. Serious, now.

RALEIGH. I'm serious, May. You're the one cuttin' up ... *(May catches her breath.)*

MAY. Now. Seriously. How would you get to school? Doctors say you can't drive. I can't take you. It's in the wrong direction.

RALEIGH. Don't you think I know that? Don't you think I know that I can't go anywhere without you drivin' me? You don't have to remind me.

MAY. I was just being practical. And honest.

RALEIGH. Well, maybe you should be sensitive sometimes instead of being practical and honest.

MAY. Raleigh, honey ...

RALEIGH. I know that I can't drive. That I'll probably never drive again. And that there aren't many jobs I can do. And it just tears me up. Sittin' on the porch all day watchin' the cars drive by and knowin' that I can't do that. Some little sixteen-year-old pimply-faced boy drivin' his girlfriend around, just for fun. Drivin' just for fun. And I can't do that for fun or work or nothin', just sit here on the porch watchin' other people drivin' around.

MAY. I'm sorry, Raleigh.

RALEIGH. No, I'm the one that's sorry. I'm a pretty sorry piece of a husband. Can't work, can't drive. Just sittin' on the porch like an old man.

MAY. I didn't know you felt that way.

RALEIGH. Well, how do you think I feel? Proud to have my wife drivin' me around? Proud to let ever'body know that my wife has to work? Proud that I live with my wife's parents?

MAY. I don't care what people think.

RALEIGH. Someday you will. Someday you'll be tired of hearin' about your lazy husband.

MAY. You're not lazy.

RALEIGH. That's what it looks like.

MAY. Since when did you care what people thought? *(A pause.)*

RALEIGH. Since I got married, I guess. *(Another pause.)*

MAY. Well.

RALEIGH. I care what people think about you.

MAY. Oh. *(May looks at Raleigh. A pause. A car horn.)*

RALEIGH. Your daddy's ready to leave.

MAY. Well, let's go then. *(May grabs her pocketbook and starts to leave down the porch steps.)*

RALEIGH. You forgot the Lemony Flat Pie.

MAY. Oh! *(May runs into the house to get the pie. Raleigh stands on the porch looking out for a moment. He exits down the steps as the lights change.)*

SCENE THREE

Early September, 1944. Afternoon. Three weeks have passed. Mrs. Gill enters from the house to cool off. She is wearing an apron and wiping her hands on a tea towel. Mrs. Brummett enters from the driveway. She is carrying a paper bag with a jar in it.

MRS. BRUMMETT. Howdy, Miz Gill. It's Miz Brummett.

MRS. GILL. Well, what a surprise. Nice to see you, Mrs. Brummett. *(Mrs. Gill notices that the tea towel she is holding is the one from Cincinnati, and she wads it in her hand.)* Come on up on the porch. I'd invite you inside, but it's too hot, too hot with all the canning. Had the stove on all day long.

MRS. BRUMMETT. It's a mighty hot September this year.

MRS. GILL. Certainly is.

MRS. BRUMMETT. I've come at a bad time.

MRS. GILL. Not at all. I was just fixin' to sit for a spell. And have a glass of iced tea. I'll get us some. Sorry it's not sweet tea. *(Mrs. Gill exits into the house, carrying the tea towel.)*

MRS. BRUMMETT. *(Loudly, calling after her.)* Don't make no trouble on my account.

MRS. GILL. *(From inside the house.)* No trouble.

MRS. BRUMMETT. *(Loudly, calling inside.)* My daughter Treva dropped me off in town this mornin'. In my son-in-law's car. With the babies. On her way to Barbourville. Told Treva to drop me at Miz Gibson's and then come get me at your place this afternoon, on her way back home. Took me a while to walk here from Main Street. Quite a hill in this heat. Treva'll be pickin' me up any time now, so I cain't stay long. Just thought it would be nice to have a visit with you a minute. Ain't seed you since Mr. Brummett's birthday. He is still laughing about that pie May brung him. *(Mrs. Gill pushes the screen door open and enters with two glasses of iced tea on a tray with a plate of cookies. She carries a different tea towel.)*

MRS. GILL. I'm sorry, I didn't hear what you said.

MRS. BRUMMETT. I said, my daughter dropped me off in town this morning. I walked up here.

MRS. GILL. Quite a hill in this heat. Here, have a seat.

MRS. BRUMMETT. Cookies. How nice. *(A beat.)* Did May make these?

MRS. GILL. No. Mr. Gill likes butter cookies. So I made some for him. They're good with tea. Sweetens it up a little. *(They sit and sip their tea.)*

MRS. BRUMMETT. Mr. Gill home?

MRS. GILL. He's back in his workshop, listening to the radio. *(A pause.)*

MRS. BRUMMETT. I won't stay long.

MRS. GILL. Not to worry.

MRS. BRUMMETT. I got to thinkin' that I ain't seed you since the birthday party, bein' as we go to different churches and all. I didn't mean to interrupt your cannin'.

MRS. GILL. Not to worry.

MRS. BRUMMETT. I was thinkin' ... Oh, I brung you a little somethin' ... *(She pulls a couple of jars from the paper bag and puts them on the table.)*

MRS. GILL. Why, thank you, Mrs. Brummett. Mighty nice.

MRS. BRUMMETT. It's pickles. It's my bread-and-butter pickles. I make 'em outa yeller squash instead of cucumbers. *(A pause.)* I hope you ain't cannin' pickles today.

MRS. GILL. No. I'm putting up jelly. I'll be sure to save you a couple of jars.

MRS. BRUMMETT. Don't go to no bother.

MRS. GILL. Plenty to go around. *(A pause.)*

MRS. BRUMMETT. Does May help you with the cannin'?

MRS. GILL. No. I do it myself.

MRS. BRUMMETT. Lot of work for one person.

MRS. GILL. Gives me something to do. It's a quiet house with the children grown.

MRS. BRUMMETT. We've got the grandbabies now. Makes for a lively scene.

MRS. GILL. I just bet it does. *(She holds out the plate.)* Cookie?

MRS. BRUMMETT. Thank you. *(Mrs. Brummett takes a cookie and nibbles on it.)* These cookies are good with the iced tea.

MRS. GILL. Yes, they are. *(They sit in silence for a while.)* Nice of you to stop by.

MRS. BRUMMETT. Nice of you to offer iced tea. Ain't nothin' better on a hot day.

MRS. GILL. Certainly ... ain't. *(They sit in silence for a while.)*

MRS. BRUMMETT. I've been meanin' to ... to ask you ... to ask you somethin'.

MRS. GILL. Please, go right ahead.

MRS. BRUMMETT. I was just wonderin' ...

MRS. GILL. Yes?

MRS. BRUMMETT. It's hard to ...

MRS. GILL. Just spill it out.

MRS. BRUMMETT. Well, you know my daughter, Treva.

MRS. GILL. Yes.

MRS. BRUMMETT. Treva has two children.

MRS. GILL. Yes. They were a handful at the birthday party.

MRS. BRUMMETT. Oh, they're always a handful. Just like Raleigh at that age. Always into somethin'. But they keep me laughin'. Nothing like grandbabies.

MRS. GILL. Yes.

MRS. BRUMMETT. Nothing like 'em. *(Mrs. Gill just sips her tea. There is a very long pause.)* I reckon I should just blurt it out.

MRS. GILL. Usually best.

MRS. BRUMMETT. I ain't heerd nothin' yet about when … about when your daughter May is, is gonna, well, my daughter, Treva, right after her weddin', was, I don't mean *right* after. It were nine months nearly t' the day. And then the second baby eleven months after that. And I got to thinkin', well, it's been over a year since Raleigh's weddin' day, and it's been on t' three months since they got back from Rock City and no one ain't mentioned anythin' to me and I was just wonderin' if there was somethin' I should know.

MRS. GILL. Perhaps you should ask your son.

MRS. BRUMMETT. I couldn't ask him a question like that.

MRS. GILL. *(Holding in a smile.)* Maybelle is not pregnant, if that's what you are wondering.

MRS. BRUMMETT. You know that fer a fact?

MRS. GILL. I don't believe they are planning on having children right away.

MRS. BRUMMETT. Babies come whether you want 'em or not.

MRS. GILL. I believe they are … taking precautions.

MRS. BRUMMETT. I don't need to know …

MRS. GILL. Since you asked.

MRS. BRUMMETT. Why would they do that? Is there somethin' wrong with May?

MRS. GILL. Actually, I believe they are concerned about Raleigh's … condition. That it might be hereditary.

MRS. BRUMMETT. Raleigh don't have no hered'ty. *(Mrs. Gill takes this in for a moment.)*

MRS. GILL. That he might pass down his epilepsy.

MRS. BRUMMETT. Oh, his little fits.

MRS. GILL. Uh-huh? *(Having an audience has loosened Mrs. Brummett's tongue.)*

MRS. BRUMMETT. Oh, he had those when he was a baby. When he didn't get his own way. He'd stop cryin' and just shake a bit, all angry like.

MRS. GILL. He had it from childhood?

MRS. BRUMMETT. Grew outta it. Babies grow outta those things, don't they? Just like his granddaddy. Git riled up over somethin' and have a fit about it. Shakin' and his eyes rollin' back. I can

33

tell you now, now that we're in-laws an' all —

MRS. GILL. Yes.

MRS. BRUMMETT. I'm sure you already know this, so I'm not tellin' tales outa school. Raleigh's ... just lazy. Don't git it from me, mind ya. He's lazy. Just readin' and writin' all the time. When he went in t' the service I thought, well, he's growed up now, but then they just sent him back, 'cause he had them fits and then the same thing happened when he tried to work in Dee-troit. *(On a roll, confiding in Mrs. Gill.)* Raleigh don't want to work, so he gets them fits. Just like when he was a baby.

MRS. GILL. Mrs. Brummett, you know that Raleigh has epilepsy.

MRS. BRUMMETT. Oh, that's what the fancy doctor told Raleigh when he took him out of the nuthouse. Six months in the nuthouse. You don't put someone in the nuthouse unless they're crazy.

MRS. GILL. It was a mistake that they placed him in the state hospital. I don't think Raleigh's crazy. Or lazy, either, for that matter.

MRS. BRUMMETT. Don't have a job, does he? Not in the service. Must be mighty hard on you, with your boy overseas.

MRS. GILL. It's nice to have Raleigh here —

MRS. BRUMMETT. *(Interrupting.)* I cain't walk down the street in Woodbine no more. I was comin' out of the drugstore and — you're not going to believe this, but it's the gospel truth — a woman spat on me. Just spat. She said my son was a coward not to go fight and that her son was killt and she spat on me. I've never, never, never seed a thing like that before. She spat on me.

MRS. GILL. Mrs. Brummett, I am so sorry to hear about that.

MRS. BRUMMETT. It was humiliatin'.

MRS. GILL. I would imagine it was.

MRS. BRUMMETT. Don't tell Raleigh nothin' 'bout it.

MRS. GILL. Of course not. I'm sure he's had his own share of that sort of thing.

MRS. BRUMMETT. Oh, he wouldn't take no notice. Just roll off his back. Just like his daddy. Nothin' bothers that boy. Always smilin' and laughin'.

MRS. GILL. He's a joy to have around. You did a good job raisin' him.

MRS. BRUMMETT. *(Bashful at the compliment.)* Did my best. *(A car horn is heard.)* Oh! That's my daughter ...

MRS. GILL. Would she like to come in?

MRS. BRUMMETT. Oh, no. Not with them babies. Got to get back and make supper. And I've interrupted your cookin'.

MRS. GILL. It was lovely of you to stop by.

MRS. BRUMMETT. Well, now that we're kin an' all.

MRS. GILL. Yes. Thanks for the visit. *(The car horn honks again. Mrs. Brummett yells toward the car, even though there is no way she could be heard.)*

MRS. BRUMMETT. I'm a comin'.

MRS. GILL. Thanks for the pickles.

MRS. BRUMMETT. Bye-bye.

MRS. GILL. Bye-bye. *(Mrs. Brummett goes toward the back of the house.)*

MRS.BRUMMETT. *(From offstage, to May.)* Bye-bye.

MAY. *(From offstage.)* Bye-bye. *(May enters, carrying a stack of papers to grade.)* What did Mrs. Brummett want? *(May begins working on her papers.)*

MRS. GILL. Brought me a jar of pickles.

MAY. Bet they're as sour as she is.

MRS. GILL. Maybelle! *(May goes back to her papers. Mrs. Gill sorts the mail. They work in silence for a minute.)* Where's Raleigh?

MAY. I don't know.

MRS. GILL. You don't know?

MAY. I just got home.

MRS. GILL. I haven't seen him all day.

MAY. I've gotta grade these papers.

MRS. GILL. Maybe he went to pick some crabapples. They're good this year.

MAY. They're sour.

MRS. GILL. Do you think? I like them a little tart. Makes a better jelly.

MAY. I wouldn't know.

MRS. GILL. You had more interest in the kitchen when you were a little girl. Always in the sugar jar. You really had a sweet tooth. You liked to help me make cookies, too.

MAY. Momma, I'm trying to grade papers.

MRS. GILL. Oh.

MAY. Polly Bartlett's husband died. I'm teaching her classes this week. Gotta grade these papers for her. *(They are quiet for a minute. Mrs. Gill sorts the mail. May works at her papers.)*

MRS. GILL. *(Rocking in her chair.)* It's a mighty good thing to have a man around the house.

MAY. Like Daddy?

MRS. GILL. Raleigh. Well, your daddy, too. We both got lucky.

MAY. I'm working, Momma. (*A pause.*)

MRS. GILL. Gonna be a nice evening. (*A pause.*) You reckon Raleigh's going to come home soon with some crabapples?

MAY. I've got to get these essays graded.

MRS. GILL. Mighty important, are they?

MAY. Yes, they are.

MRS. GILL. Mighty important.

MAY. Reckon so.

MRS. GILL. Most important thing in the world right now?

MAY. Momma.

MRS. GILL. More important than knowing where your husband is? (*May looks at her mother. Without speaking she collects the papers and takes them into the house. Mrs. Gill keeps rocking. May comes back out, carrying her sweater. She takes the car keys out of her purse as she starts down the steps.*) Going for a drive?

MAY. Yep.

MRS. GILL. Be back for supper. It's Raleigh's favorite tonight. (*May exits toward the driveway. Mrs. Gill rocks for a minute, stops, picks up half the sorted mail and starts to exit into the house. Raleigh enters from the side yard opposite where May exited.*) Lawsy day. I just sent May off looking for you.

RALEIGH. Reckon she'll find me eventually.

MRS. GILL. I got worried. Not like you to be gone all day.

RALEIGH. Out with my sister.

MRS. GILL. Well, that's nice, then. I've got to get back to making your supper.

RALEIGH. Anything I can do?

MRS. GILL. Not a thing. Not a thing I can think of. (*Mrs. Gill exits into the house with the tray and the pickles. Raleigh lights a cigarette. He sits on the porch, staring out. As the lights change, he puts out the cigarette, but remains sitting.*)

SCENE FOUR

An hour later. May enters from the driveway. May is angry, but can't raise her voice, for fear of being heard by her mother.

MAY. *(To Raleigh.)* Where've you been?

RALEIGH. Just talkin' to your momma.

MAY. Where were you before that?

RALEIGH. Around back in the workshop talkin' with your daddy.

MAY. Where've you been all day long?

RALEIGH. Barbourville.

MAY. Why didn't you tell me you were going to Barbourville?

RALEIGH. Didn't decide 'til you'd already left.

MAY. How'd you get to Barbourville?

RALEIGH. My sister drove me. I hitched back. Thought I'd beat you home, but it took a while to get a ride.

MAY. You went all the way to Barbourville without telling me?

RALEIGH. Didn't know I had to report in to you every day. Thought I was out of the service.

MAY. I was worried. You could've ... could've had a ... had a seizure or something.

RALEIGH. Haven't had one in almost two years.

MAY. But you could. You could have a seizure on the road somewhere and no one would know. You need to tell me where you're going.

RALEIGH. What're you so riled up about? Just went to Barbourville. With my sister.

MAY. It scared me. You gone. When Momma said she hadn't seen you all day I got this cold feeling.

RALEIGH. You're just tired, Maisy. Reckon you need some supper.

MAY. Reckon I do.

RALEIGH. Set a spell. *(May sits. They are silent for a moment.)*

MAY. So when do you start school?

RALEIGH. I don't.

MAY. Isn't that why you went to Barbourville? To enroll?

RALEIGH. Yep.

MAY. But you decided not to go?

RALEIGH. They decided for me.

MAY. What do you mean?

RALEIGH. Don't you have papers to grade? I'll tell you later. *(Raleigh starts to leave.)* Raleigh. You tell me

MAY. Tell me now. *(Raleigh starts to leave.)* Raleigh. You tell me what happened.

RALEIGH. They don't have room for me. That's it. They don't have room for me. *(Raleigh again turns to leave.)*

MAY. Raleigh Brummett, you sit right down here and talk to your wife. *(After a beat, Raleigh sits.)*

RALEIGH. All the GI's heading back. You have to have served ninety days to qualify.

MAY. You served three months.

RALEIGH. Nope. I got medical discharge after eighty-two days. I signed up and it doesn't even count. The GI's get preferred, preferential treatment, they call it. Not just preferred, but that's all they have room for. I don't get to go. I don't get to go to college. They won't take me. So that's it.

MAY. But you're a published writer. Don't they know that?

RALEIGH. They don't care. Well, they said they were sorry, but they can't do anything about it. All comes from the admissions office. So I'm not gonna go to school, May. Just like you wanted. You happy now? I'm going back the workshop.

MAY. You stay here and talk to me.

RALEIGH. I have been talking to you. I told you what you wanted to know. I'm not gonna go to school.

MAY. So what are you going to do?

RALEIGH. I'm gonna go see your daddy in the workshop.

MAY. I didn't mean —

RALEIGH. I know what you meant! I'm gonna go out t' the back and think about what I'm gonna do.

MAY. There are other schools —

RALEIGH. It will be the same everywhere. The boys that fought get first placement. And all paid for, too, by Uncle Sam. Some semi-illiterate farmboys getting a college education now, just because they went and killed some other boys in Europe. Those farmboys didn't even sign up. They got drafted. I signed up. I signed up. I didn't wait to get drafted. I volunteered. I was ready to go fight, but Uncle Sam said I couldn't. Uncle Sam said I couldn't go fight and now they're telling me I can't get a college degree. *(He looks at May.)* Don't you have anything to say?

MAY. I'm sorry, Raleigh. It's so unfair.

RALEIGH. Unfair? *(May comes close to Raleigh to comfort him.)*
MAY. You smell like smoke. You've been smoking? When did you start smoking?
RALEIGH. Since my whole life fell apart. Since I got stuck here with nothing to do.
MAY. It's just a little hard patch.
RALEIGH. What would you know? You've had it so easy. Smart enough to get a scholarship.
MAY. You're smart.
RALEIGH. Breeze right through school. Get a job right away. Had it so easy.
MAY. I have not.
RALEIGH. When haven't you? Your daddy a carpenter with a nice little farm. No coal miners in your family. No sharecroppers. Just easy, easy.
MAY. I've been working. Most wives at home.
RALEIGH. You wanting to stay home, May? Let me support you?
MAY. Well, no, I don't.
RALEIGH. That's a good thing, May. A very good thing. And do you know why? Because I don't have a job. I can't support you. I can't support you. I can't even do factory work without the blinkin' lights causing a seizure. I can't drive a car. I can't drive a tractor. If you weren't workin' we'd be starvin'. I can't even feed my wife. It's a good thing we don't have a family, because they'd be starvin'.
MAY. Our kids wouldn't starve.
RALEIGH. Might not have a choice.
MAY. My daddy would …
RALEIGH. Your daddy. Your daddy. Your daddy always took care of you. But now you have a husband, May. And a husband's supposed to look after you. To feed you. To support you. And I'm not doing that.
MAY. I don't care.
RALEIGH. Well, I do. I care. *(A pause.)* I'm going for a walk.
MAY. I'll go with you.
RALEIGH. Don't you have papers to grade?
MAY. I can do them later.
RALEIGH. *(Overlapping.)* Get your work done, May. *(Raleigh starts to leave.)*
MAY. Don't you walk out of here. Don't you walk out on me. *(Raleigh is gone. Mrs. Gill enters from the house.)*
MRS. GILL. Where's Raleigh?

MAY. Gone for a walk.

MRS. GILL. Where'd he go?

MAY. *(Sharply.)* Nowhere. He's goin' nowhere.

MRS. GILL. You don't give that boy enough credit. Thinking about yourself all the time. *(May throws down the papers, scattering them on the porch floor.)* You got a bee in your bonnet? *(May runs into the house, slamming the door behind her. Mrs. Gill picks up the papers and follows May into the house, as the lights change.)*

SCENE FIVE

In the transition we hear radio reports of Victory in Europe. The following spring, May, 1945. Late afternoon. Raleigh comes from around the side yard. He lights a cigarette and smokes for a minute, staring out. Mrs. Gill enters from the house. She is carrying a package.

MRS. GILL. Don't let May catch you smoking.

RALEIGH. You mind?

MRS. GILL. Not if it's outside. My daddy raised tobacco. Cigarette smells good sometimes. Reminds me of my daddy. When I'm gathering the eggs I stop by the window, the back window of the workshop. I can smell Mr. Gill's cigarette. Reminds me of my daddy. That smell of fresh-cut lumber and cigarettes. Don't tell Mr. Gill. He thinks I don't know that he smokes back there. I tell him it's dangerous with all the sawdust. But it smells right good. *(Raleigh stands on the steps and smokes. Mrs. Gill sits back down. A car drives by.)*

RALEIGH. Ford.

MRS. GILL. Have you ever seen so many cars driving around? Nice to have so much gasoline again.

RALEIGH. Yep.

MRS. GILL. Got a letter from Charlie today.

RALEIGH. Find out exactly where he is?

MRS. GILL. No. Just happy to get a letter.

RALEIGH. What's he asking for this time?

MRS. GILL. What makes you think he's asking for anything?

RALEIGH. 'Cause every time you get a letter you send him a

package.

MRS. GILL. I do?

RALEIGH. You sure do.

MRS. GILL. Well, he'll be home soon. This'll be the last package. The very last one.

RALEIGH. Yep. Over before we know it.

MRS. GILL. I've missed him.

RALEIGH. I know you have. *(Mrs. Gill points to some letters on the table.)*

MRS. GILL. Yonder's some mail for you, too.

RALEIGH. I don't think Charlie's writing me. It's just more rejection letters. *(A pause. A car drives by. Looking out:)* '36 Chrysler.

MRS. GILL. Sure is. We used to have one just like it. Never liked that car. *(Another pause.)* I'll put your mail in the trash for you, then. *(Mrs. Gill starts to leave with the mail.)*

RALEIGH. That's okay. You can just leave the mail on the table.

MRS. GILL. No bother.

RALEIGH. I'll pitch them out later.

MRS. GILL. On my way. No bother a'tall.

RALEIGH. I'll toss 'em.

MRS. GILL. I'm takin' out the trash anyway. Pick-up day's tomorrow.

RALEIGH. I'll take out the trash for you.

MRS. GILL. Not to worry. You rest your feet. Looks like you've had a long day. *(Mrs. Gill gathers up Raleigh's mail.)*

RALEIGH. Well, just let me take just a quick look then. *(Mrs. Gill hands Raleigh the mail. Mrs. Gill sits. Raleigh quickly goes through the mail. He glances at the return address on one envelope and opens it quickly. He reads it twice.)* Well, looky here.

MRS. GILL. Somebody wanting one of your stories?

RALEIGH. No. But it's a letter from Maxwell Perkins.

MRS. GILL. *(Not knowing who this is.)* Friend of yours? *(Raleigh laughs.)*

RALEIGH. Nope. Sure would like him to be, though. He's F. Scott Fitzgerald's editor.

MRS. GILL. Why's he writing you?

RALEIGH. Wants to meet me. Maxwell Perkins wants to meet me in New York City. In his office.

MRS. GILL. — my word —

RALEIGH. He wants me to take the train to New York City.

MRS. GILL. Then that's what you should do. *(A pause.)*

RALEIGH. Trains are all full. Soldiers get priority. There aren't any seats.

MRS. GILL. You could stand.

RALEIGH. He wants to see a novel. He's looking for novels.

MRS. GILL. Then write a novel and take it to him.

RALEIGH. Well, truth is, novels don't pay much. Not like stories. And nobody's buying my stories anymore. I wouldn't have anything to show somebody like Maxwell Perkins. I've never written a novel.

MRS. GILL. So write one.

RALEIGH. Write a novel. Just like that. I don't even have an idea for a novel.

MRS. GILL. A novel's just a big story, isn't it?

RALEIGH. What am I gonna write about? If I can't write stories that sell I sure can't write a novel worth anything.

MRS. GILL. Write about ... about dogs. People always like stories about dogs.

RALEIGH. I don't know any dogs. Just the old hounds my Uncle Clyde used to hunt with.

MRS. GILL. What about them?

RALEIGH. Might make a story. Uncle Clyde and his cronies would sit top their hill just listenin' to the dogs chase the rabbits. They knew when a dog was after something by the way it howled. Might make a story. But I can't write a novel about it.

MRS. GILL. We had a dog went to church.

RALEIGH. To church?

MRS. GILL. Liked to embarrass Maybelle to death. That's why she started going to First Methodist.

RALEIGH. You took the dog to church?

MRS. GILL. Oh, no. He would follow us. To Felts Chapel. Jimbo. That was his name. When we'd be walking to church he'd follow. Well, Jimbo got to knowing we didn't want him to go. So he'd take off early and go on ahead of us, because he knew about what time we'd be leaving. He knew when Sunday was, because he'd see us, I guess, dressed differently than we were during the week.

RALEIGH. Different shoes. Smell of the shoes.

MRS. GILL. Probably. And that Mr. Gill was still here and hadn't gone to work. Well, Jimbo would go across the highway and wait for us up the hill. And when we'd get closer he'd go a little further, so when we'd get to Felts Chapel he'd already be there. He would slip in when someone would open the door and he'd go all the way up to the front, where there was a pot belly stove and he'd get up close to that stove. And some of them at church said he was there whether we were there or not.

RALEIGH. No.

MRS. GILL. Yessiree. And Maybelle was always embarrassed, him going into church. She'd say, well, I'm not going to church if that dog is gonna be there. Oh, we'd start putting him up, Charlie'd catch him and put him up the night before. Jimbo got wise to that. He would leave, he would figure out the time we were gonna start looking for him, we'd try to put him in a little shed we had. But he'd go on down the road and spend the night, across the highway, and we couldn't find him. And the next morning we'd go to church and there he'd be. And in the summertimes he'd go to the tent meetings with us, come home with sawdust all over him. Maybelle got so she wouldn't go to church with us anymore, because of Jimbo. She started going to First Methodist downtown. One day they had a missionary speak to them, and next thing you know she's wanting to be a missionary, too, and so she goes to Asbury College. Sure made me real happy when she married you.

RALEIGH. Why, thank you.

MRS. GILL. That Jimbo. He'd sleep through the singing, but when the preacher started the sermon, I swear, that dog was listening to every word. (A beat.) Jimbo wanted to go to church and that's what he did. And nobody was going to stop him. (A pause, as Raleigh takes this in.)

RALEIGH. Thanks, Momma Gill.

MRS. GILL. For what? (Raleigh smiles at her and goes inside with the mail. A car is heard entering the driveway and stopping. Mrs. Gill rereads her letter from Charlie. May enters.) Got a letter from Charlie!

MAY. Good. (A pause.)

MRS. GILL. You're home early.

MAY. Yes.

MRS. GILL. Nice to be home early for a change. (May doesn't answer. A pause.) I'm off to the post office. The last package to Charlie. The very last one! Home before you know it! My boy is coming home.

MAY. Yes.

MRS. GILL. You work too many hours. Good of you to let the children out early for V-E day.

MAY. They already got a day off for that.

MRS. GILL. Oh, that's right.

MAY. They already got a day off.

MRS. GILL. I just can't keep track of your schedule.

MAY. The district meeting was today.

MRS. GILL. I just can't keep track of —

MAY. You don't need to keep track of my schedule, Momma.

MRS. GILL. Just want to have supper on the table for Raleigh.

MAY. You don't have to do that.

MRS. GILL. Well, someone has to. *(Unseen by the two women, at some point during the following dialogue, Raleigh appears from the side yard.)*

MAY. Maybe Raleigh —

MRS. GILL. I like doing it.

MAY. Maybe Raleigh should learn to cook. Maybe Raleigh should fix his own supper.

MRS. GILL. Gives me something to do.

MAY. Maybe Raleigh should find something to — what are we gonna do, Momma?

MRS. GILL. We're gonna celebrate.

MAY. I don't mean that.

MRS. GILL. Your brother is gonna come home soon and we're gonna celebrate. Aren't you happy the war's gonna be over?

MAY. You're right, Momma. Of course you're right. There's nothing better in the world than to have Charlie back home. *(Mrs. Gill sees Raleigh.)*

MRS. GILL. Raleigh, would you like to ride to town with me?

MAY. Yes, he would.

RALEIGH. No. Thanks.

MRS. GILL. *(To May.)* I've got a roast cooking for supper tonight. That roast just needs to simmer a little more. I'll be back for supper. Roast tonight! Guess you know why! *(Mrs. Gill exits toward the driveway. May and Raleigh stare at each other. Raleigh hears a car and looks toward the road.)*

MAY. Don't say it.

RALEIGH. What?

MAY. Don't you dare say it.

RALEIGH. Say what?

MAY. If I hear "Plymouth" or "Chrysler" out of your mouth one more time I'm gonna scream. I am. I really am. I don't care. I don't care if it's a Model T, even. Don't have to keep telling me. I can see there's a car driving by. And I don't care. If you were a dog you'd be chasing after them. If you were a dog you'd be chasing the cars down the road barking at them.

RALEIGH. I do something?

MAY. You don't do something. You don't do anything. You just sit around all day. *(May sits, staring at the road. A car is heard. May glares at Raleigh. Raleigh returns her stare. As the car drives past, Raleigh begins barking at it.)*

RALEIGH. Grrrr ... ruff! Ruff! Ruff!

MAY. That's not funny.

RALEIGH. Oh, that's right. You don't like dogs. *(Raleigh starts to leave.)*

MAY. '33 Plymouth. We used to have one like it.

RALEIGH. Nope. It's a '32. Tell by the taillight.

MAY. Oh, you're right.

RALEIGH. Four cylinder. '32.

MAY. Ours was a year old when we got it. *(They stare out at the road. Silence.)*

RALEIGH. Roads slick this mornin'?

MAY. Not a bit.

RALEIGH. Thought they'd be slick this morning.

MAY. No, they weren't.

RALEIGH. I was a mite concerned.

MAY. No need.

RALEIGH. Rained last night. Thought the roads'd be slick.

MAY. Dry as a bone. I got to school early.

RALEIGH. Good. *(Silence. A car drives by. Both of them see it, but neither comments on it.)* You gonna tell me what's eatin' you?

MAY. I'm just tired. The district meeting was today.

RALEIGH. That'll wear anybody out.

MAY. What would you know about it?

RALEIGH. Better go check on that roast.

MAY. You telling me what to do?

RALEIGH. No, I'm not. I meant I was gonna take a look at it.

MAY. I'll do it.

RALEIGH. You're tired.

MAY. You stay right here.

RALEIGH. And have you keep snappin' at me? You don't like dogs, well, I don't like snappin' turtles. *(A car drives by. Raleigh forces himself not to look. May bursts into tears.)* Are you gonna tell me what happened at the meeting?

MAY. All those men, they don't know a single blessèd thing about my school. Some just back from the war. What do they know about what's been going on back here?

RALEIGH. Probably not much.

45

MAY. All they do is trade war stories.

RALEIGH. Sounds like a useless meetin'.

MAY. It was. It was useless. It was the most useless meeting ever.

RALEIGH. What happened?

MAY. It's ... I don't know ... They're gonna ... it's a ... a ... structure, they called it. I'm gonna ... And Margaret Shirley's not retiring until after another school year. Another whole year.

RALEIGH. Slow down. Start at the beginnin' and tell me what happened at the meetin'.

MAY. They talk about the war for about half an hour. Finally they stop. The superintendent's just sitting there looking at me. We're gonna adjust the structuring, he said. What's that, I ask.

RALEIGH. Slow down and catch your breath.

MAY. I think he's talking about building a new building or something.

RALEIGH. What is it?

MAY. That's what I asked, what kind of structure? Well, they said, reassignments. Paint Lick's going to have a new principal. A new principal.

RALEIGH. Paint Lick Element'ry?

MAY. Both. The high school and the element'ry.

RALEIGH. What did you say?

MAY. I must have been sitting there with my mouth just, just hanging open, I was so shocked.

RALEIGH. I just bet you were.

MAY. Last meeting they told me, the superintendent told me, what a good job I was doing and all.

RALEIGH. I remember.

MAY. So I'm thinking, oh, they must be transferring me. And the thoughts are just flying through my head — what are you and I going to do, will we have to move, will it be more money.

RALEIGH. Don't worry about —

MAY. And then the ... And the superintendent says to me, well, the war's almost over, and the boys are coming home so you can go be a housewife now, as if that were something I should really want to do. *(Straight to Raleigh.)* I didn't mean it that way. I didn't mean —

RALEIGH. Just tell me what happened.

MAY. I said what do you mean? I still didn't get it. And they looked at each other and sort of nodded, all fake-sympathetic. I have good news, he said. You won't have to work so hard, anymore. I told him I don't mind working hard. *(Straight to Raleigh.)* I don't.

RALEIGH. You work hard.

MAY. I do. I work very hard.

RALEIGH. And they know that.

MAY. Wasn't about that. He said again, the war's over. And I said, I know the war's over and that means there'll be more boys at school now. But I can handle them. Don't worry about that. And they laughed and one of them, a fat ole guy said, I'm sure you can, little lady. And I still didn't get what they were telling me. The war's over. The war's over. What's that mean? We're all happy about that. I was thinking all this as I was just staring at them. As if they'd asked me some question I couldn't answer.

RALEIGH. Take it easy.

MAY. And they said, well, the superintendent said, our boys are back now, and they need jobs.

RALEIGH. Oh.

MAY. Yes. David Johnson's going to be the new principal at the school. What school will I be at, I asked. You'll be ... they look at a piece of paper as if they didn't know already. You'll be replacing, if you want to, Margaret Shirley.

RALEIGH. Margaret Shirley?

MAY. She'll be retiring. Teaches second grade.

RALEIGH. Well, that's something.

MAY. Second grade. And not for another year, even. She's retiring, but not for at least another year, maybe two.

RALEIGH. Oh.

MAY. Then they said, if you want to come back. Want to come back, I asked. Where am I going? They smiled and said with a year off you'll probably be starting a family, won't you. That's my business, I said. No, we have to make it our business, they said. We're giving all the principal and assistant principal jobs to returning soldiers. The ones old enough to have been in college are officers and they'll make good principals and we have to support our boys who fought for us. And I was just trying not to cry.

RALEIGH. Did you cry?

MAY. Not then. Not right then.

RALEIGH. That's my Maisy. *(Raleigh takes out his notebook and writes in it.)*

MAY. They've taken away my job. *(Raleigh keeps writing.)* Did you hear me? I don't have a job. What're we gonna do?

RALEIGH. *(As he's writing.)* We'll manage, Maisy.

MAY. You're just wearing rose-colored glasses. I don't have a job.

How am I going to take care of you?

RALEIGH. Is that what you think this marriage is about? Maisy, don't worry. *(Raleigh puts his notebook in his pocket.)* Everything's under control. *(May bursts into tears. Raleigh puts his arms around her. She sobs for a minute.)* Gonna be a full moon tonight.

MAY. So?

RALEIGH. Looks like a good night for a moonbow over Cumberland Falls. It's gonna be our anniversary tomorrow.

MAY. It is? I forgot!

RALEIGH. You forgot marryin' me?

MAY. Silly.

RALEIGH. Best day of my life. So what'dya say you and I take a drive over to the State Park?

MAY. Momma made a roast for supper.

RALEIGH. Roast is better on the second day.

MAY. I don't want to drive — it'll be dark.

RALEIGH. That's the idea. See the moonbow over Cumberland Falls. *(A pause, as May considers.)*

MAY. If you want to.

RALEIGH. Mighty fine then. And you know what?

MAY. What?

RALEIGH. I got a letter from a big New York editor today.

MAY. You did?

RALEIGH. And you know what else?

MAY. No, what?

RALEIGH. I'm gonna start a novel.

MAY. You are?

RALEIGH. Yep. We can do anything, Maisy. I'm gonna write a novel. You'll get another job. Where else was there ever a high school principal young as you?

MAY. Wouldn't've happened if it weren't for the war.

RALEIGH. But you did it! You were the principal. We're amazing, Maisy. And soon as the war's over, and it can't be long now, soon as the war's over and your brother's back, we'll have our own house, in town, or even in Lexington, somewhere I can walk to the library. Our own home and we'll have people over and talk about life and books and things. It's gonna be wonderful, Maisy. I reckon we are the two luckiest people in Laurel County. The luckiest people in America. Maybe in the world, even. *(A beat.)* We've got each other. We've got everything we need. *(A pause.)* Happy anniversary, Maisy.

MAY. Happy anniversary.

RALEIGH. So let's go to Cumberland Falls. I'm gonna tell you all about my new novel. Just now I got the best idea for a novel. The best ever. And guess what else? You're gonna be in it. You're gonna be the heroine in my novel.

MAY. Me?

RALEIGH. You.

MAY. Tell me now.

RALEIGH. Nope. I'll tell you at Cumberland Falls. Grab the car keys and let's go. *(May smiles at Raleigh. Mrs. Gill enters from the driveway, returning with the unmailed package, a telegram in her hand. Without speaking, she slowly climbs the steps and looks at May. She crosses the porch and goes into the house. May and Raleigh look at each other as the realization of the telegram sinks in.)*

MAY. Momma? Momma? Momma! *(May runs into the house. Perhaps we hear "No!" and sobbing. Raleigh looks out at the road for a minute. He watches a car go by, but doesn't say anything. As the lights change he turns and slowly goes into the house, as if dreading what he's going to find inside.)*

SCENE SIX

In the transition we hear radio reports of the atomic bombing of Hiroshima, or perhaps a portion of Truman's speech on August ninth. Several months later. August, 1945. Early evening. Raleigh enters from the house. He sits and watches the road. May enters from the house, drying her hands on the Cincinnati tea towel, which by now has faded quite a bit.

RALEIGH. Good supper, May.

MAY. No it wasn't. It wasn't very good. Not as good as Momma makes.

RALEIGH. Hit the spot.

MAY. I wish Momma would start cooking again. She's just sitting in the back yard all the time. Goes and stands by the window by the workshop. It's strange.

RALEIGH. She'll be all right. She's strong like you.

MAY. Like me? You think I'm strong?

RALEIGH. Sure do.

MAY. Hmmm. *(A pause.)* Why does she always stand by the work-shop window?

RALEIGH. Just wants to be close to your daddy I reckon.

MAY. Without bothering him?

RALEIGH. Yep. She's a smart woman.

MAY. But she's stopped cooking.

RALEIGH. Just give her some time.

MAY. That's what Daddy says.

RALEIGH. He's a clever man.

MAY. Never realized before how much like him you are.

RALEIGH. You think? I take that as a compliment.

MAY. It is. *(They sit in silence for a moment.)* You listen to the radio today?

RALEIGH. Yep.

MAY. I just couldn't.

RALEIGH. They'll surrender any day now. It's pretty much over.

MAY. You think we'll drop another one?

RALEIGH. I think two was enough.

MAY. Can't get my mind around it.

RALEIGH. Yep.

MAY. Wonder what Roosevelt would've done.

RALEIGH. Hard to know.

MAY. Daddy sure loved Roosevelt.

RALEIGH. Your daddy and I had a long talk today.

MAY. About what?

RALEIGH. Real good talk. I'm thinking about — *(Looking out.)* Looky there.

MAY. What?

RALEIGH. My sister's car.

MAY. Your momma in it?

RALEIGH. Yep.

MAY. Probably bringing more food.

RALEIGH. Probably.

MAY. You got some more work to do? I'll talk to her.

RALEIGH. Nope. I'm finished for today. That mule tired me out. Fighting me every inch of the field. I think I'd rather face my mom than look at the backside of that mule again.

MAY. Maybe she won't stay long.

RALEIGH. *(Waving.)* Howdy, Mom.

MAY. *(Waving.)* Mom Brummett. *(Mrs. Brummett enters from*

50

around the side driveway, carrying a covered dish. At some point in the scene May notices the tea towel and folds it so Mrs. Brummett can't see the word "Cincinnati.")

MRS. BRUMMETT. I brought you all some cooked squash. Takin' over the garden this year. We've got mor'n we can eat. Cain't stay, but wanted to bring by a dish.

MAY. You've already brought us —

MRS. BRUMMETT. Times of trouble, gotta hep each other out, don't we?

RALEIGH. Thanks, Mom.

MRS. BRUMMETT. It'll be good for your supper tonight. I cain't stay, but your daddy'll like it.

MAY. We've already —

RALEIGH. *(Interrupting.)* Thanks, Mom.

MRS. BRUMMETT. I cain't stay. Your sister'll be right back t' pick me up. She's droppin' a dish at the Gibson's. Cooked rhubarb. Miz Gibson lost her son last week.

RALEIGH. Mighty kind of you, Mom.

MRS. BRUMMETT. We've gotta hep each other out. And we had so much of that rhubarb. Mr. Brummett don't like it a-tall. I don't know why Treva planted it. Them children won't touch it, neither. Raleigh, you take this dish in t' Miz Gill. *(Raleigh starts to leave.)* Oh, and will you bring out my pie plate and the yeller mixin' bowl that I brung the potato salad in day afore yesterday?

MAY. We enjoyed the potato salad.

MRS. BRUMMETT. It's right good, ain' it? Them sweet pickles in it 's what makes it so tasty. And a little mustard. *(Raleigh goes inside, leaving May alone with Mrs. Brummett.)* I'm sorry 'bout your brother.

MAY. Yes.

MRS. BRUMMETT. The good Lord works in mysterious ways.

MAY. Yes.

MRS. BRUMMETT. I reckon your momma's grievin' pretty hard.

MAY. She's a strong woman.

MRS. BRUMMETT. Takes faith to get through thangs like this.

MAY. Yes, it does.

MRS. BRUMMETT. Now, I know you and your family are saved, and that gives me comfort as I'm sure it does you.

MAY. Everybody at church has been —

MRS. BRUMMETT. We just have t' trust that our maker has his own plans for us. I know you're grievin' pretty hard for your brother right now, but the Lord doesn't give us more than we can bear.

MAY. Maybe I should help Raleigh find your pie plate.

MRS. BRUMMETT. You know, Mr. Brummett traveled for the railroad before he got crippled an' couldn't work no more. Folks said it were jake leg, but I knowed he wasn't a drinkin' man. The Lord just put his finger on him and made him crippled. The Lord can heal and the Lord can cause afflictions. And he caused my husband to be crippled. But you don't hear me complaining. I always look on the bright side of things.

MAY. Mom Brummett —

MRS. BRUMMETT. It's a blessing they don't need you at that school no more, 'cause your momma and your daddy need you here at home. *(May is biting her lip, trying not to get mad at Mrs. Brummett. We see her maturity. A car horn is heard.)* We all have our crosses to bear. Raleigh's never gonna to amount to nothin'. That's your cross. Raleigh's never gonna to amount to nothin'. And now that your brother's not comin' back, it's up to you to help your daddy run his farm. That's all I have to say.

MAY. Thank you, Mom Brummett.

MRS. BRUMMETT. You're right welcome. I'll be prayin' fer you. *(Raleigh enters from the house.)*

RALEIGH. These your dishes, Mom?

MRS. BRUMMETT. That's them. Thanks.

RALEIGH. Thanks for bringin' them.

MRS. BRUMMETT. Glad I could help. *(A car horn is heard.)* Bye-bye. *(Mrs. Brummett exits. There is a pause.)*

MAY. You didn't tell my momma that your momma was here, did you?

RALEIGH. Nope.

MAY. Thought you didn't. *(A pause.)*

RALEIGH. Talked to your daddy today. Building construction'll be picking up again soon. He wants to get back to cabinet making.

MAY. That's good to hear.

RALEIGH. Maybe furniture. People always need furniture.

MAY. Yes.

RALEIGH. People'll be wanting to start over now. Start families. Reckon there'll be a good market for cabinets and furniture.

MAY. Yes.

RALEIGH. Thought I'd work with him.

MAY. What?

RALEIGH. Thought I'd go into business with your daddy. We've been talking about it.

MAY. You can't … operate machinery.

RALEIGH. I could stain and varnish. Your daddy can teach me how to do the fine finishing. *(May ponders this. There is a very long pause.)* Saw a brand-new Cadillac today. Nice car, Cadillac. *(A pause.)*

MAY. I reckon you need to find … to find something interesting to do.

RALEIGH. I'm gonna be busy working with your daddy.

MAY. What about your writing?

RALEIGH. I'll get back to writing stories someday. *(A pause.)*

MAY. Person's got to have something to do.

RALEIGH. Yep. I'm lucky to work with your daddy.

MAY. I mean someplace to go. I had my teaching. And now, well, right now I'm taking care of my momma and my daddy and my husband, looking after all of you, but you … you …

RALEIGH. I'm not complaining, May.

MAY. I know you're not. And I appreciate that. I really do appreciate that. *(A pause.)* I recollect you were real happy when we were in Cincinnati.

RALEIGH. It was a real happy time.

MAY. It was.

RALEIGH. Even if you didn't get to Lookout Mountain?

MAY. I'd forgotten about that!

RALEIGH. Someday, when I sell another story, I'm gonna take you to see Rock City! A second honeymoon.

MAY. I thought our first one was pretty special.

RALEIGH. Happy memories.

MAY. You liked being in a city. You liked the city.

RALEIGH. So did you.

MAY. 'Cause I was with you. But if I had been there alone it wouldn't have been much fun.

RALEIGH. It was fun with you.

MAY. *(A pause.)* You were … you were … inspired somehow. By being in a city.

RALEIGH. It was different.

MAY. You joined up the service before anyone was being drafted, even.

RALEIGH. I could see what was coming.

MAY. You wanted … you needed … to go someplace different. When I first met you, on the train, you were on your way to New York City, right?

RALEIGH. I was thinkin' about it.

MAY. You had already thought about it. You were on your way to New York City.

RALEIGH. Maybe I was.

MAY. And you came back home to Kentucky because you met me.

RALEIGH. I don't rightly recollect.

MAY. I do. And you're staying here because of me.

RALEIGH. Kentucky's my home, May.

MAY. But this house isn't a home for you. For us. Someday we need a home of our own.

RALEIGH. Someday we'll have one.

MAY. But right now ...

RALEIGH. May, what are you driving at?

MAY. You need ... I can't believe I'm saying this, even. You need to be someplace else. You need to be in a city. Maybe New York City, even. Find out about your writing. Meet the people that buy your stories. That editor you were talking about. They'd buy more stories if they could meet you, wouldn't they? If they got to know you. I think you should go try out New York City. I think ... I think ... I think ... you ... you ... you'd sort of ... maybe find yourself there. Find out what you were really meant to do. I was meant to teach. And I knew that from the time I was fifteen years old, teaching Sunday school. I thought that I'd be a missionary and go teach, but things didn't work out that way, and here I am. But you ... you ... haven't even had a chance to find out what's out there for you and I was thinking maybe you should.

RALEIGH. May, are you telling me we should move to New York City? *(May thinks for a minute.)*

MAY. No. Guess not. Just thinking.

RALEIGH. All righty. *(Silence.)*

MAY. *(An idea coming to her.)* But ... but ... I think ... *you.* I think *you* should.

RALEIGH. I should what?

MAY. You should ... go try it out, maybe.

RALEIGH. By myself.

MAY. I reckon. *(A pause.)* I have to stay here. I can't leave my momma right now. Not with Charlie just killed. I can't leave my momma and my daddy. *(A pause.)* I know my place is next to you, you're my husband, and I should be with you and cooking for you, but for right now I think I have to stay here and I think you should go try out New York City. *(A pause.)* And I reckon you've been thinking the same thing. *(Raleigh is silent.)* Maybe you just need a little pushing.

RALEIGH. You think?

MAY. I've just been waiting for you to tell me when you're going.

RALEIGH. You're full of surprises, Maisy.

MAY. Reckon life is full of surprises.

RALEIGH. Reckon it is. *(They sit in silence for a very long time.)*

MAY. When's the next train to New York City?

RALEIGH. There's one every day. Goes through Cincinnati. *(They both register "Cincinnati." There is a pause.)*

MAY. There's one tomorrow?

RALEIGH. I can catch one next week.

MAY. There's a train tomorrow?

RALEIGH. Yes, there is. *(Raleigh holds May close. They kiss. May breaks the embrace. She is stoic.)*

MAY. You best be going before our mommas talk us out of it. Best be packing.

RALEIGH. Best be. *(Raleigh turns to go inside.)* Don't have much to pack. Just some books, maybe.

MAY. Buy yourself some new clothes in New York City.

RALEIGH. My clothes are fine. Reckon those city folks better like me just the way I am.

MAY. I reckon they will. What do you think it's like in New York City?

RALEIGH. Lots of tall buildings, I hear.

MAY. No trees?

RALEIGH. I don't think so. Just lots of tall buildings. Like big ole rocks. *(They embrace. Mrs. Gill comes out the door. She walks to the edge of the porch. All are silent. Raleigh turns to go into the house.)*

MRS. GILL. Oh, I'm disturbing you.

RALEIGH. Not a bit. I was just leaving. Just gonna take care of somethin'. *(Raleigh goes inside. Mrs. Gill stands, staring out at the road. May sits on the glider. She looks at her mother.)*

MAY. Come sit with me, Momma. *(Mrs. Gill slowly walks over and sits down next to May. She looks out at the road. May stares out, too, as the lights fade to black.)*

End of Play

PROPERTY LIST

Homemade birdhouse
Suitcases
Drinking glasses or period tumblers
Pitcher of lemonade
Tray
New tea towel from Cincinnati
Same tea towel faded
Covered pie plate
Another tea towel
Mail
Plate of cookies
Pitcher of iced tea
Papers
Grading book
Application form
Pencil
Notebook
Jar of pickles
Covered dish
Pie plate
Yellow bowl

Mrs. Brummett's Yellow Squash Pickles

9 cups finely sliced yellow squash or zucchini
2 cups finely sliced onions
1 Tbsp salt

Combine squash and onions in a bowl.
Sprinkle with the salt and let stand one hour.

½ cup diced green pepper
1 cup cider vinegar
1 ½ (to 1 ¾) cups sugar
½ tsp. celery seed
5 tsp. mustard seed (the round yellow seeds)
1 tsp. turmeric

Combine green pepper, vinegar, sugar and seasonings; bring to boil.

Add squash and onion mixture. Return to a boil and cook five minutes.

Pack in sterile jars. Cover with seasoned liquid and seal.

Process in water bath for five minutes.

This makes three pints.

Playwright's note: The above is a family recipe, very close to my grandmother's "bread and butter" pickles that I liked so much as a child. The directions call for 1 ¾ cups sugar; I like less. The secret to these pickles is to use long skinny squash and to slice it paper-thin. The green pepper should be in small cubes. Be careful not to boil the mixture too long so that the vegetables are still a little crunchy. If you plan to serve these right away and refrigerate the leftovers, you can skip the canning. Enjoy.

NEW PLAYS

★ **THE EXONERATED by Jessica Blank and Erik Jensen.** Six interwoven stories paint a picture of an American criminal justice system gone horribly wrong and six brave souls who persevered to survive it. "The #1 play of the year...intense and deeply affecting..." –*NY Times.* "Riveting. Simple, honest storytelling that demands reflection." –*A.P.* "Artful and moving...pays tribute to the resilience of human hearts and minds." –*Variety.* "Stark...riveting...cunningly orchestrated." –*The New Yorker.* "Hard-hitting, powerful, and socially relevant." –*Hollywood Reporter.* [7M, 3W] ISBN: 0-8222-1946-8

★ **STRING FEVER by Jacquelyn Reingold.** Lily juggles the big issues: turning forty, artificial insemination and the elusive scientific Theory of Everything in this Off-Broadway comedy hit. "Applies the elusive rules of string theory to the conundrums of one woman's love life. Think *Sex and the City* meets *Copenhagen.*" –*NY Times.* "A funny offbeat and touching look at relationships...an appealing romantic comedy populated by oddball characters." –*NY Daily News.* "Where kooky, zany, and madcap meet...whimsically winsome." –*NY Magazine.* "STRING FEVER will have audience members happily stringing along." –*TheaterMania.com.* "Reingold's language is surprising, inventive, and unique." –*nytheatre.com.* "...[a] whimsical comic voice." –*Time Out.* [3M, 3W (doubling)] ISBN: 0-8222-1952-2

★ **DEBBIE DOES DALLAS adapted by Erica Schmidt, composed by Andrew Sherman, conceived by Susan L. Schwartz.** A modern morality tale told as a comic musical of tragic proportions as the classic film is brought to the stage. "A scream! A saucy, tongue-in-cheek romp." –*The New Yorker.* "Hilarious! DEBBIE manages to have it all: beauty, brains and a great sense of humor!" –*Time Out.* "Shamelessly silly, shrewdly self-aware and proud of being naughty. Great fun!" –*NY Times.* "Racy and raucous, a lighthearted, fast-paced thoroughly engaging and hilarious send-up." –*NY Daily News.* [3M, 5W] ISBN: 0-8222-1955-7

★ **THE MYSTERY PLAYS by Roberto Aguirre-Sacasa.** Two interrelated one acts, loosely based on the tradition of the medieval mystery plays. "... stylish, spine-tingling...Mr. Aguirre-Sacasa uses standard tricks of horror stories, borrowing liberally from masters like Kafka, Lovecraft, Hitchcock...But his mastery of the genre is his own...irresistible." –*NY Times.* "Undaunted by the special-effects limitations of theatre, playwright and *Marvel* comic-book writer Roberto Aguirre-Sacasa maps out some creepy twilight zones in THE MYSTERY PLAYS, an engaging, related pair of one acts...The theatre may rarely deliver shocks equivalent to, say, *Dawn of the Dead,* but Aguirre-Sacasa's work is fine compensation." –*Time Out.* [4M, 2W] ISBN: 0-8222-2038-5

★ **THE JOURNALS OF MIHAIL SEBASTIAN by David Auburn.** This epic one-man play spans eight tumultuous years and opens a uniquely personal window on the Romanian Holocaust and the Second World War. "Powerful." –*NY Times.* "[THE JOURNALS OF MIHAIL SEBASTIAN] allows us to glimpse the idiosyncratic effects of that awful history on one intelligent, pragmatic, recognizably real man..." –*NY Newsday.* [3M, 5W] ISBN: 0-8222-2006-7

★ **LIVING OUT by Lisa Loomer.** The story of the complicated relationship between a Salvadoran nanny and the Anglo lawyer she works for. "A stellar new play. Searingly funny." –*The New Yorker.* "Both generous and merciless, equally enjoyable and disturbing." –*NY Newsday.* "A bitingly funny new comedy. The plight of working mothers is explored from two pointedly contrasting perspectives in this sympathetic, sensitive new play." –*Variety.* [2M, 6W] ISBN: 0-8222-1994-8

DRAMATISTS PLAY SERVICE, INC.
440 Park Avenue South, New York, NY 10016 212-683-8960 Fax 212-213-1539
postmaster@dramatists.com www.dramatists.com

NEW PLAYS

★ **MATCH by Stephen Belber.** Mike and Lisa Davis interview a dancer and choreographer about his life, but it is soon evident that their agenda will either ruin or inspire them—and definitely change their lives forever. "Prolific laughs and ear-to-ear smiles." *–NY Magazine.* "Uproariously funny, deeply moving, enthralling theater. Stephen Belber's MATCH has great beauty and tenderness, and abounds in wit." *–NY Daily News.* "Three and a half out of four stars." *–USA Today.* "A theatrical steeplechase that leads straight from outrageous bitchery to unadorned, heartfelt emotion." *–Wall Street Journal.* [2M, 1W] ISBN: 0-8222-2020-2

★ **HANK WILLIAMS: LOST HIGHWAY by Randal Myler and Mark Harelik.** The story of the beloved and volatile country-music legend Hank Williams, featuring twenty-five of his most unforgettable songs. "[LOST HIGHWAY has] the exhilarating feeling of Williams on stage in a particular place on a particular night...serves up classic country with the edges raw and the energy hot...By the end of the play, you've traveled on a profound emotional journey: LOST HIGHWAY transports its audience and communicates the inspiring message of the beauty and richness of Williams' songs...forceful, clear-eyed, moving, impressive." *–Rolling Stone.* "...honors a very particular musical talent with care and energy... smart, sweet, poignant." *–NY Times.* [7M, 3W] ISBN: 0-8222-1985-9

★ **THE STORY by Tracey Scott Wilson.** An ambitious black newspaper reporter goes against her editor to investigate a murder and finds the *best* story...but at what cost? "A singular new voice...deeply emotional, deeply intellectual, and deeply musical..." *–The New Yorker.* "...a conscientious and absorbing new drama..." *–NY Times.* "...a riveting, tough-minded drama about race, reporting and the truth..." *–A.P.* "... a stylish, attention-holding script that ends on a chilling note that will leave viewers with much to talk about." *–Curtain Up.* [2M, 7W (doubling, flexible casting)] ISBN: 0-8222-1998-0

★ **OUR LADY OF 121st STREET by Stephen Adly Guirgis.** The body of Sister Rose, beloved Harlem nun, has been stolen, reuniting a group of life-challenged childhood friends who square off as they wait for her return. "A scorching and dark new comedy... Mr. Guirgis has one of the finest imaginations for dialogue to come along in years." *–NY Times.* "Stephen Guirgis may be the best playwright in America under forty." *–NY Magazine.* [8M, 4W] ISBN: 0-8222-1965-4

★ **HOLLYWOOD ARMS by Carrie Hamilton and Carol Burnett.** The coming-of-age story of a dreamer who manages to escape her bleak life and follow her romantic ambitions to stardom. Based on Carol Burnett's bestselling autobiography, *One More Time.* "...pure theatre and pure entertainment..." *–Talkin' Broadway.* "...a warm, fuzzy evening of theatre." *–BrodwayBeat.com.* "...chuckles and smiles of recognition or surprise flow naturally...a remarkable slice of life." *–TheatreScene.net.* [5M, 5W, 1 girl] ISBN: 0-8222-1959-X

★ **INVENTING VAN GOGH by Steven Dietz.** A haunting and hallucinatory drama about the making of art, the obsession to create and the fine line that separates truth from myth. "Like a van Gogh painting, Dietz's story is a gorgeous example of excess—one that remakes reality with broad, well-chosen brush strokes. At evening's end, we're left with the author's resounding opinions on art and artifice, and provoked by his constant query into which is greater: van Gogh's art or his violent myth." *–Phoenix New Times.* "Dietz's writing is never simple. It is always brilliant. Shaded, compressed, direct, lucid—he frames his subject with a remarkable understanding of painting as a physical experience." *–Tucson Citizen.* [4M, 1W] ISBN: 0-8222-1954-9

DRAMATISTS PLAY SERVICE, INC.
440 Park Avenue South, New York, NY 10016 212-683-8960 Fax 212-213-1539
postmaster@dramatists.com www.dramatists.com

NEW PLAYS

★ **INTIMATE APPAREL by Lynn Nottage.** The moving and lyrical story of a turn-of-the-century black seamstress whose gifted hands and sewing machine are the tools she uses to fashion her dreams from the whole cloth of her life's experiences. "…Nottage's play has a delicacy and eloquence that seem absolutely right for the time she is depicting…" *—NY Daily News.* "…thoughtful, affecting…The play offers poignant commentary on an era when the cut and color of one's dress—and of course, skin—determined whom one could and could not marry, sleep with, even talk to in public." *—Variety.* [2M, 4W] ISBN: 0-8222-2009-1

★ **BROOKLYN BOY by Donald Margulies.** A witty and insightful look at what happens to a writer when his novel hits the bestseller list. "The characters are beautifully drawn, the dialogue sparkles…" *—nytheatre.com.* "Few playwrights have the mastery to smartly investigate so much through a laugh-out-loud comedy that combines the vintage subject matter of successful writer-returning-to-ethnic-roots with the familiar mid-life crisis." *—Show Business Weekly.* [4M, 3W] ISBN: 0-8222-2074-1

★ **CROWNS by Regina Taylor.** Hats become a springboard for an exploration of black history and identity in this celebratory musical play. "Taylor pulls off a Hat Trick: She scores thrice, turning CROWNS into an artful amalgamation of oral history, fashion show, and musical theater…" *—TheatreMania.com.* "…wholly theatrical…Ms. Taylor has created a show that seems to arise out of spontaneous combustion, as if a bevy of department-store customers simultaneously decided to stage a revival meeting in the changing room." *—NY Times.* [1M, 6W (2 musicians)] ISBN: 0-8222-1963-8

★ **EXITS AND ENTRANCES by Athol Fugard.** The story of a relationship between a young playwright on the threshold of his career and an aging actor who has reached the end of his. "[Fugard] can say more with a single line than most playwrights convey in an entire script…Paraphrasing the title, it's safe to say this drama, making its memorable entrance into our consciousness, is unlikely to exit as long as a theater exists for exceptional work." *—Variety.* "A thought-provoking, elegant and engrossing new play…" *—Hollywood Reporter.* [2M] ISBN: 0-8222-2041-5

★ **BUG by Tracy Letts.** A thriller featuring a pair of star-crossed lovers in an Oklahoma City motel facing a bug invasion, paranoia, conspiracy theories and twisted psychological motives. "…obscenely exciting…top-flight craftsmanship. Buckle up and brace yourself…" *—NY Times.* "…[a] thoroughly outrageous and thoroughly entertaining play…the possibility of enemies, real and imagined, to squash has never been more theatrical." *—A.P.* [3M, 2W] ISBN: 0-8222-2016-4

★ **THOM PAIN (BASED ON NOTHING) by Will Eno.** An ordinary man muses on childhood, yearning, disappointment and loss, as he draws the audience into his last-ditch plea for empathy and enlightenment. "It's one of those treasured nights in the theater—treasured nights anywhere, for that matter—that can leave you both breathless with exhilaration and…in a puddle of tears." *—NY Times.* "Eno's words…are familiar, but proffered in a way that is constantly contradictory to our expectations. Beckett is certainly among his literary ancestors." *—nytheatre.com.* [1M] ISBN: 0-8222-2076-8

★ **THE LONG CHRISTMAS RIDE HOME by Paula Vogel.** Past, present and future collide on a snowy Christmas Eve for a troubled family of five. "…[a] lovely and hauntingly original family drama…a work that breathes so much life into the theater." *—Time Out.* "…[a] delicate visual feast…" *—NY Times.* "…brutal and lovely…the overall effect is magical." *—NY Newsday.* [3M, 3W] ISBN: 0-8222-2003-2

DRAMATISTS PLAY SERVICE, INC.
440 Park Avenue South, New York, NY 10016 212-683-8960 Fax 212-213-1539
postmaster@dramatists.com www.dramatists.com